Benjamin Wood

Fort Lafayette

A Novel

Benjamin Wood

Fort Lafayette
A Novel

ISBN/EAN: 9783337052751

Printed in Europe, USA, Canada, Australia, Japan

Cover: Foto ©ninafisch / pixelio.de

More available books at **www.hansebooks.com**

FORT LAFAYETTE;

OR,

LOVE AND SECESSION.

A Novel,

BY BENJAMIN WOOD.

NEW YORK:
Carleton, Publisher, 413 Broadway,
(LATE, RUDD & CARLETON).
MDCCCLXII.

———" Whom they please they lay in basest bonds."
Venice Preserved.

———•••———

" O, beauteous Peace!
   Sweet union of a state! what else but thou
   Gives safety, strength, and glory to a people?"
Thomson.

" Oh, Peace! thou source and soul of social life;
   Beneath whose calm inspiring influence,
   Science his views enlarges, art refines,
   And swelling commerce opens all her ports;
   Blest be the man divine, who gives us thee!"
Thomson.

" A peace is of the nature of a conquest;
   For then both parties nobly are subdued,
   And neither party loser."
Shakspeare.

FORT LAFAYETTE;

OR,

LOVE AND SECESSION.

CHAPTER I.

There is a pleasant villa on the southern bank of the James River, a few miles below the city of Richmond. The family mansion, an old fashioned building of white stone, surrounded by a spacious veranda, and embowered among stately elms and grave old oaks, is sure to attract the attention of the traveller by its picturesque appearance, and the dreamy elegance and air of comfort that pervade the spot. The volumes of smoke that roll from the tall chimneys, the wide portals of the hall, flung open as if for a sign of welcome, the merry chat and cheerful faces of the sable household, lazily alternating their domestic labors with a sly romp or a lounge in some quiet nook, these and other traits of the old Virginia home, complete the picture of hospitable affluence which the stranger instinctively draws as his gaze lingers on the grateful scene. The house stands on a wooded knoll, within a bowshot of the river bank, and from the steps of the back veranda, where creeping flowers form a perfumed network of a thousand hues, the velvety lawn shelves gracefully down to the water's edge.

Toward sunset of one of the early days of April, 1861, a young girl stood leaning upon the wicket of a fence which separated the garden from the highway. She stood there dreamily gazing along the road, as if awaiting the approach of some one who would be welcome when he came. The slanting rays of the declining sun glanced through the honeysuckles and tendrils that intertwined among the white palings, and threw a subdued light upon her face. It was a face that was beautiful in repose, but that promised to be more beautiful when awakened into animation. The large, grey eyes were half veiled with their black lashes at that moment, and their expression was thoughtful and subdued; but ever as the lids were raised, when some distant sound arrested her attention, the expression changed with a sudden flash, and a gleam like an electric fire darted from the glowing orbs. Her features were small and delicately cut, the nostrils thin and firm, and the lips most exquisitely molded, but in the severe chiselling of their arched lines betraying a somewhat passionate and haughty nature. But the rose tint was so warm upon her cheek, the raven hair clustered with such luxuriant grace about her brows, and the *petite* and lithe figure was so symmetrical at every point, that the impression of haughtiness was lost in the contemplation of so many charms.

Oriana Weems, the subject of our sketch, was an orphan. Her father, a wealthy Virginian, died while his daughter was yet an infant, and her mother, who had been almost constantly an invalid, did not long survive. Oriana and her brother, Beverly, her senior by two years, had thus been left at an early age in the charge of their mother's sister, a maiden lady of excellent heart and quiet disposition, who certainly had most conscientiously fulfilled the sacred trust. Oriana had returned but a twelvemonth before from a northern seminary, where she had gathered up more accomplishments than she would ever be likely to make use of in the old homestead; while Beverly, having graduated at Yale the preceding month, had written to his sister that she might expect him that very day, in company with his classmate and friend, Arthur Wayne.

She stood, therefore, at the wicket, gazing down the road, in expectation of catching the first glimpse of her brother and his friend, for whom horses had been sent to Richmond, to await their arrival at the depot. So much was she absorbed in revery, that she failed to observe a solitary horseman who approached from the opposite direction. He plodded leisurely along until within a few feet of the wicket, when he quietly drew rein and gazed for a moment in silence upon the unconscious girl. He was a tall, gaunt man, with stooping shoulders, angular features, lank, black hair and a sinister expression, in which cunning and malice combined. He finally urged his horse a step nearer, and as softly as his rough voice would admit, he bade: "Good evening, Miss Oriana."

She started, and turned with a suddenness that caused the animal he rode to swerve. Recovering her composure as suddenly, she slightly inclined her head and turning from him, proceeded toward the house.

"Stay, Miss Oriana, if you please."

She paused and glanced somewhat haughtily over her shoulder.

"May I speak a word with you?"

"My aunt, sir, is within; if you have business, I will inform her of your presence."

"My business is with you, Miss Weems," and, dismounting, he passed through the gate and stepped quickly to her side.

"Why do you avoid me?"

Her dark eye flashed in the twilight, and she drew her slight form up till it seemed to gain a foot in height.

"We do not seek to enlarge our social circle, Mr. Rawbon. You will excuse me if I leave you abruptly, but the night dew begins to fall."

She moved on, but he followed and placed his

hand gently on her arm. She shook it off with more of fierceness than dignity, and the man's eyes fairly sought the ground beneath the glance she gave him.

"You know that I love you," he said, in a hoarse murmur, "and that's the reason you treat me like a dog."

She turned her back upon him, and walked, as if she heard him not, along the garden path. His brow darkened, and quickening his pace, he stepped rudely before her and blocked the way.

"Look you, Miss Weems, you have insulted me with your proud ways time and time again, and I have borne it tamely, because I loved you, and because I've sworn that I shall have you. It's that puppy, Harold Hare, that has stepped in between you and me. Now mark you," and he raised his finger threateningly, "I won't be so meek with him as I've been with you."

The girl shuddered slightly, but recovering, walked forward with a step so stately and commanding, that Rawbon, bold and angry as he was, involuntarily made way for her, and she sprang up the steps of the veranda and passed into the hall. He stood gazing after her for a moment, nervously switching the rosebush at his side with his heavy horsewhip; then, with a muttered curse, he strode hastily away, and leaping upon his horse, galloped furiously down the road.

Seth Rawbon was a native of Massachusetts, but for some ten years previously to the date at which our tale commences, he had been mostly a resident of Richmond, where his acuteness and active business habits had enabled him to accumulate an independent fortune. His wealth and vigorous progressive spirit had given him a certain degree of influence among the middle classes of the community, but his uncouth manner, and a suspicion that he was not altogether free from the degradation of slave-dealing, had, to his great mortification and in spite of his persistent efforts, excluded him from social intercourse with the aristocracy of the Old Dominion. He was not a man, however, to give way to obstacles, and with characteristic vanity and self-reliance, he had, shortly after her return from school, greatly astonished the proud Oriana with a bold declaration of love and an offer of his hand and fortune. Not intimidated by a sharp and decidedly ungracious refusal, he had at every opportunity advocated his hopeless suit, and with so much persistence and effrontery, that the object of his unwelcome passion had been goaded from indifference to repugnance and absolute loathing. Harold Hare, whose name he had mentioned with so much bitterness in the course of the interview we have represented, was a young Rhode Islander, who had, upon her brother's invitation, sojourned a few weeks at the mansion some six months previously, while on his way to engage in a surveying expedition in Western Virginia. He had promised to return in good time, to join Beverly and his guest, Arthur Wayne, at the close of their academic labors.

A few moments after Rawbon's angry departure, the family carriage drove rapidly up to the hall door, and the next instant Beverly was in his sister's arms, and had been affectionately welcomed by his old-fashioned, kindly looking aunt. As he turned to introduce his friend, Arthur, the latter was gazing with an air of

absent admiration upon the kindled features of
Oriana. The two young men were of the same
age, apparently about one-and-twenty; but in
character and appearance they were widely
different. Beverly was, in countenance and
manner, curiously like his sister, except that the
features were bolder and more strongly marked.
Arthur, on the contrary, was delicate in feature
almost to effeminacy. His brow was pale and
lofty, and above the auburn locks were massed
like a golden coronet. His eyes were very large
and blue, with a peculiar softness and sadness
that suited well the expression of thoughtfulness
and repose about his lips. He was taller than
his friend, and although well-formed and graceful, was slim and evidently not in robust health.
His voice, as he spoke in acknowledgment of
the introduction, was low and musical, but
touched with a mournfulness that was apparent
even in the few words of conventional courtesy
that he pronounced.

Having thus domiciliated them comfortably
in the old hall, we will leave them to recover
from the fatigues of the journey, and to taste of
the plentiful hospitalities of Riverside manor.

CHAPTER II.

Early in the fresh April morning, the party at Riverside manor were congregated in the hall, doing full justice to Aunt Nancy's substantial breakfast.

"Oriana," said Beverly, as he paused from demolishing a well-buttered batter cake, and handed his cup for a second supply of the fragrant Mocha, "I will leave it to your *savoir faire* to transform our friend Arthur into a thorough southerner, before we yield him back to his Green Mountains. He is already half a convert to our institutions, and will give you not half so much trouble as that obstinate Harold Hare."

She slightly colored at the name, but quietly remarked:

"Mr. Wayne must look about him and judge from his own observation, not my arguments. I certainly do not intend to annoy him during his visit, with political discussions."

"And yet you drove Harold wild with your flaming harangues, and gave him more logic in an afternoon ride than he had ever been bored with in Cambridge in a month."

"Only when he provoked and invited the assault," she replied, smiling. "But I trust, Mr. Wayne, that the cloud which is gathering above our country will not darken the sunshine of your visit at Riverside manor. It is unfortunate that you should have come at an unpropitious moment, when we cannot promise you that perhaps there will not be some cold looks here and there among the townsfolk, to give you a false impression of a Virginia welcome."

"Not at all, Oriana; Arthur will have smiles and welcome enough here at the manor house to make him proof against all the hard looks in Richmond. I prevailed on him to come at all hazards, and we are bound to have a good time and don't want you to discourage us; eh, Arthur?"

"I am but little of a politician, Miss Weems," said Arthur, "although I take our country's differences much at heart. I shall surely not provoke discussion with you, like our friend

Harold, upon an unpleasant subject, while you give me *carte blanche* to enjoy your conversation upon themes more congenial to my nature."

She inclined her head with rather more of gravity than the nature of the conversation warranted, and her lips were slightly compressed as she observed that Arthur's blue eyes were fixed pensively, but intently, on her face.

The meal being over, Oriana and Wayne strolled on the lawn toward the river bank, while the carriage was being prepared for a morning drive. They stood on the soft grass at the water's edge, and as Arthur gazed with a glow of pleasure at the beautiful prospect before him, his fair companion pointed out with evident pride the many objects of beauty and interest that were within view on the opposite bank.

"Are you a sailor, Mr. Wayne? If so, we must have out the boat this afternoon, and you will find some fairy nooks beyond the bend that will repay you for exploring them, if you have a taste for a lovely waterscape. I know you are proud of the grand old hills of your native State, but we have something to boast of too in our Virginia scenery."

"If you will be my helmswoman, I can imagine nothing more delightful than the excursion you propose. But I am inland bred, and must place myself at the mercy of your nautical experience."

"Oh, I am a skillful captain, Mr. Wayne, and will make a good sailor of you before you leave us. Mr. Hare will tell you that I am to be trusted with the helm, even when the wind blows right smartly, as it sometimes does even on that now placid stream. But with his memories of the magnificent Hudson, he was too prone to quiz me about what he called our pretty rivulet. You know him, do you not?"

"Oh, well. He was Beverly's college-mate and mine, though somewhat our senior."

"And your warm friend, I believe?"

"Yes, and well worthy our friendship. Somewhat high-tempered and quick-spoken, but with a heart—like your brother's, Miss Weems, as generous and frank as a summer day."

"I do not think him high-tempered beyond the requisites of manhood," she replied, with something like asperity in her tone. "I cannot endure your meek, mild mannered men, who seem to forget their sex, and almost make me long to change my own with them, that their sweet dispositions may be better placed."

He glanced at her with a somewhat surprised air, that brought a slight blush to her cheek; but he seemed unconscious of it, and said, almost mechanically:

"And yet, that same high spirit, which you prize so dearly, had, in his case, almost caused you a severe affliction."

"What do you mean?"

"Have you not heard how curiously Beverly's intimacy with Harold was brought about? And yet it was not likely that he should have told you, although I know no harm in letting you know."

She turned toward him with an air of attention, as if in expectation.

"It was simply this. Not being class-mates, they had been almost strangers to each other at college, until, by a mere accident, an argument respecting your Southern institutions led to an angry dispute, and harsh words passed between them. Being both of the ardent temperament you so much admire, a challenge ensued, and, in spite of my entreaty and remonstrance, a duel. Your brother was seriously wounded, and Harold, shocked beyond expression, knelt by his side as he lay bleeding on the sward, and bitterly accusing himself, begged his forgiveness, and, I need not add, received it frankly. Harold was unremitting in his attentions to your brother during the period of his illness, and from the day of that hostile meeting, the most devoted friendship has existed between them. But it was an idle quarrel, Miss Weems, and was near to have cost you an only brother."

She remained silent for a few moments, and was evidently affected by the recital. Then she spoke, softly as if communing with herself: "Harold is a brave and noble fellow, and I thank God that he did not kill my brother!" and a bright tear rolled upon her cheek. She dashed it away, almost angrily, and glancing steadily at Arthur:

"Do you condemn duelling?"

"Assuredly."

"But what would you have men do in the

face of insult? Would you not have fought under the same provocation?"

"No, nor under any provocation. I hold too sacred the life that God has given. With God's help, I shall not shed human blood, except in the strict line of necessity and duty."

"It is evident, sir, that you hold your own life most sacred," she said, with a curl of her proud lip that was unmistakable.

She did not observe the pallor that overspread his features, nor the expression, not of anger, but of anguish, that settled upon his face, for she had turned half away from him, and was gazing vacantly across the river. There was an unpleasant pause, which was broken by the noise of voices in alarm near the house, the trampling of hoofs, and the rattle of wheels.

The carriage had been standing at the door, while Beverly was arranging some casual business, which delayed him in his rooms. While the attention of the groom in charge had been attracted by some freak of his companions, a little black urchin, not over five years of age, had clambered unnoticed into the vehicle, and seizing the long whip, began to flourish it about with all his baby strength. The horses, which were high bred and spirited, had become impatient, and feeling the lash, started suddenly, jerking themselves free from the careless grasp of the inattentive groom. The sudden shout of surprise and terror that arose from the group of idle negroes, startled the animals into a gallop, and they went coursing, not along the road, but upon the lawn, straight toward the river bank, which, in the line of their course, was precipitous and rocky. As Oriana and Arthur turned at the sound, they beheld the frightened steeds plunging across the lawn, and upon the carriage seat the little fellow who had caused the mischief was crouching bewildered and helpless, and screaming with affright. Oriana clasped her hands, and cried tearfully:

"Oh! poor little Pomp will be killed!"

In fact the danger was imminent, for the lawn at that spot merged into a rocky space, forming a little bluff which overhung the stream some fifteen feet. Oriana's hand was laid instinctively upon Arthur's shoulder, and with the other she pointed, with a gesture of bewildered anxiety, at the approaching vehicle. Arthur paused only long enough to understand the situation, and then stepping calmly a few paces to the left, stood directly in the path of the rushing steeds.

"Oh, Mr. Wayne! no, no!" cried Oriana, in a tone half of fear and half supplication; but he stood there unmoved, with the same quiet, mournful expression that he habitually wore. The horses faltered somewhat when they became conscious of this fixed, calm figure directly in their course. They would have turned, but their impetus was too great, and they swerved only enough to bring the head of the off horse in a line with Arthur's body. As coolly as if he was taking up a favorite book, but with a rapid movement, he grasped the rein below the bit with both hands firmly, and swung upon it with his whole weight. The frightened animal turned half round, stumbled, and rolled upon his side, his mate falling upon his knees beside him; the carriage was overturned with a crash, and little Pompey pitched out upon the greensward, unhurt.

By this time, Beverly, followed by a

crowd of excited negroes, had reached the spot.

"How is it, Arthur," said Beverly, placing his hand affectionately on his friend's shoulder, "are you hurt?"

"No," he replied, the melancholy look softening into a pleasant smile; but as he rose and adjusted his disordered dress, he coughed painfully—the same dry, hacking cough that had often made those who loved him turn to him with an anxious look. It was evident that his delicate frame was ill suited to such rough exercise.

"We shall be cheated out of our ride this morning," said Beverly, "for that axle has been less fortunate than you, Arthur; it is seriously hurt."

They moved slowly toward the house, Oriana looking silently at the grass as she walked mechanically at her brother's side. When Arthur descended into the drawing-room, after having changed his soiled apparel, he found her seated there alone, by the casement, with her brow upon her hand. He sat down at the table and glanced abstractedly over the leaves of a scrap-book. Thus they sat silently for a quarter hour, when she arose, and stood beside him.

"Will you forgive me, Mr. Wayne?"

He looked up and saw that she had been weeping. The haughty curl of the lip and proud look from the eye were all gone, and her expression was of humility and sorrow. She held out her hand to him with an air almost of entreaty. He raised it respectfully to his lips, and with the low, musical voice, sadder than ever before, he said:

"I am sorry that you should grieve about anything. There is nothing to forgive. Let us forget it."

"Oh, Mr. Wayne, how unkind I have been, and how cruelly I have wronged you!"

She pressed his hand between both her palms for a moment, and looked into his face, as if studying to read if some trace of resentment were not visible. But the blue eyes looked down kindly and mournfully upon her, and bursting into tears, she turned from him, and hurriedly left the room.

CHAPTER III.

The incident related in the preceding chapter seemed to have effected a marked change in the demeanor of Oriana toward her brother's guest. She realized with painful force the wrong that her thoughtlessness, more than her malice, had inflicted on a noble character, and it required all of Arthur's winning sweetness of disposition to remove from her mind the impression that she stood, while in his presence, in the light of an unforgiven culprit. They were necessarily much in each other's company, in the course of the many rambles and excursions that were devised to relieve the monotony of the old manor house, and Oriana was surprised to feel herself insensibly attracted toward the shy and pensive man, whose character, so far as it was betrayed by outward sign, was the very reverse of her own impassioned temperament. She discovered that the unruffled surface covered an under-current of pure thought and exquisite feeling, and when, on the bosom of the river, or in the solitudes of the forest, his spirit threw off its reserve under the spell of nature's inspiration, she felt her own impetuous organization rebuked and held in awe by the simple and quiet grandeur that his eloquence revealed.

One afternoon, some two weeks after his arrival at the Riverside manor, while returning from a canter in the neighborhood, they paused upon an eminence that overlooked a portion of the city of Richmond. There, upon an open space, could be seen a great number of the citizens assembled, apparently listening to the harangue of an orator. The occasional cheer that arose from the multitude faintly reached their ears, and that mass of humanity, restless, turbulent and excited, seemed, even at that distance, to be swayed by some mighty passion.

"Look, Miss Weems," said Arthur, "at this magnificent circle of gorgeous scenery, that you are so justly proud of, that lies around you in the golden sunset like a dream of a fairy landscape. See how the slanting rays just tip the crest of that distant ridge, making it glow like a coronet of gold, and then, leaping into the river beneath, spangle its bosom with dazzling sheen, save where a part rests in the purple shadow of the mountain. Look to the right, and see how those crimson clouds seem bending from heaven to kiss the yellow corn-fields that stretch along the horizon. And at your feet, the city of Richmond extends along the valley."

"We admit the beauty of the scene and the accuracy of the description," said Beverly, "but, for my part, I should prefer the less romantic view of some of Aunt Nancy's batter-cakes, for this ride has famished me."

"Now look below," continued Arthur, "at that swarm of human beings clustering together like angry bees. As we stand here gazing at the glorious pageant which nature spreads out before us, one might suppose that only for some festival of rejoicing or thanksgiving would men assemble at such an hour and in such a scene. But what are the beauties of the landscape, bathed in the glories of the setting-sun, to them? They have met to listen to words of passion and bitterness, to doctrines of strife, to denunciations and criminations against their fellow-men. And, doubtless, a similar scene of freemen invoking the spirit of contention that we behold yonder in that pleasant valley of the Old Dominion, is being enacted at the North and at the South, at the East and at the West, all over the length and breadth of our country. The seeds of discord are being carefully and persistently gathered and disseminated, and on both sides, these erring mortals will claim to be acting in the name of patriotism. Beverly, do you surmise nothing ominous of evil in that gathering?"

"Ten to one, some stirring news from Charleston. We must ride over after supper, Arthur, and learn the upshot of it."

"And I will be a sybil for the nonce," said Oriana, with a kindling eye, "and prophecy that Southern cannon have opened upon Sumter."

In the evening, in despite of a threatening sky, Arthur and Beverly mounted their horses and galloped toward Richmond. As they approached the city, the rain fell heavily and they sought shelter at a wayside tavern. Observing the public room to be full, they passed into a private parlor and ordered some slight refreshment. In the adjoining tap-room they could hear the voices of excited men, discussing some topic of absorbing interest. Their anticipations were realized, for they quickly gathered from the tenor of the disjointed conversation that the bombardment of Fort Sumter had begun.

"I'll bet my pile," said a rough voice, "that the gridiron bunting won't float another day in South Carolina."

"I'll go you halves on that, hoss, and you and I won't grow greyer nor we be, before Old Virginny says ' me too.' "

" Seth Rawbon, you'd better be packing your traps for Massachusetts. She'll want you afore long."

" Boys," ejaculated the last-mentioned personage, with an oath, " I left off being a Massachusetts man twelve years ago. I'm with *you*, and you know it. Let's drink. Boys, here's to spunky little South Carolina; may she go in and win! Stranger, what'll you drink?"

" I will not drink," replied a clear, manly voice, which had been silent till then.

" And why will you not drink?" rejoined the other, mocking the dignified and determined tone in which the invitation was refused.

" It is sufficient that I will not."

"Mayhap you don't like my sentiment?"

"Right."

"Look you, Mr. Harold Hare, I know you well, and I think we'll take you down from your high horse before you're many hours older in these parts. Boys, let's make him drink to South Carolina."

"Who is he, anyhow?"

"He's an abolitionist; just the kind that'll look a darned sight more natural in a coat of tar and feathers. Cut out his heart and you'll find John Brown's picture there as large as life."

At the mention of Harold's name, Arthur and Beverly had started up simultaneously, and throwing open the bar-room door, entered hastily. Harold had risen from his seat and stood confronting Rawbon with an air in which anger and contempt were strangely blended. The latter leaned with awkward carelessness against the counter, sipping a glass of spirits and water with a malicious smile.

"You are an insolent scoundrel," said Harold, "and I would horsewhip you, if you were worth the pains."

Rawbon looked around and for a second seemed

to study the faces of those about him. Then lazily reaching over toward Harold, he took him by the arm and drew him toward the counter.

"Say, you just come and drink to South Carolina."

The heavy horsewhip in Harold's hand rose suddenly and descended like a flash. The knotted lash struck Rawbon full in the mouth, splitting the lips like a knife. In an instant several knives were drawn, and Rawbon, spluttering an oath through the spurting blood that choked his utterance, drew a revolver from its holster at his side.

The entrance of the two young men was timely. They immediately placed themselves in front of Harold, and Arthur, with his usual mild expression, looked full in Rawbon's eye, although the latter's pistol was in a line with his breast.

"Stand out of the way, you two," shouted Rawbon, savagely.

"What is the meaning of this, gentlemen?" said Beverly, quietly, to the excited bystanders, to several of whom he was personally known

"Squire Weems," replied one among them, "you had better stand aside. Rawbon has a lien on that fellow's hide. He's an abolitionist, anyhow, and ain't worth your interference."

"He is my very intimate friend, and I will answer for him to any one here," said Beverly, warmly.

"I will answer for myself," said Hare, pressing forward.

"Then answer that!" yelled Rawbon, levelling and shooting with a rapid movement. But Wayne's quiet eye had been riveted upon him all the while, and he had thrown up the ruffian's arm as he pulled the trigger.

Beverly's eyes flashed like live coals, and he sprang at Rawbon's throat, but the crowd pressed between them, and for a while the utmost confusion prevailed, but no blows were struck. The landlord, a sullen, black-browed man, who had hitherto leaned silently on the counter, taking no part in the fray, now interposed.

"Come, I don't want no more loose shooting here!" and, by way of assisting his remark, he took down his double-barrelled shot-gun and jumped upon the counter. The fellow was well known for a desperate though not quarrelsome character, and his action had the effect of somewhat quieting the excited crowd.

"Boys," continued he, "it's only Yankee against Yankee, anyhow; if they're gwine to fight, let the stranger have fair play. Here stranger, if you're a friend of Squire Weems, you kin have a fair show in my house, I reckon, so take hold of this," and taking a revolver from his belt, he passed it to Beverly, who cocked it and slipped it into Harold's hand. Rawbon, who throughout the confusion had been watching for the opportunity of a shot at his antagonist, now found himself front to front with the object of his hate, for the bystanders had instinctively drawn back a space, and even Wayne and Weems, willing to trust to their friend's coolness and judgment, had stepped aside.

Harold sighted his man as coolly as if he had been aiming at a squirrel. Rawbon did not flinch, for he was not wanting in physical courage, but he evidently concluded that the chances were against him, and with a bitter smile, he walked slowly toward the door. Turning at the threshold, he scowled for a moment at Harold, as if hesitating whether to accept the encounter.

"I'll fix you yet," he finally muttered, and left the room. A few moments afterward, the three friends were mounted and riding briskly toward Riverside manor.

CHAPTER IV.

Oriana, after awaiting till a late hour the return of her brother and his friend, had retired to rest, and was sleeping soundly when the party entered the house, after their remarkable adventure. She was therefore unconscious, upon descending from her apartment in the morning, of the addition to her little household. Standing upon the veranda, she perceived what she supposed to be her brother's form moving among the shrubbery in the garden. She hastened to accost him, curious to ascertain the nature of the excitement in Richmond on the preceding afternoon. Great was her astonishment and unfeigned her pleasure, upon turning a little clump of bushes, to find herself face to face with Harold Hare.

He had been lost in meditation, but upon seeing her his brow lit up as a midnight sky brightens when a passing cloud has unshrouded the full moon. With a cry of joy she held out both her hands to him, which he pressed silently for a moment as he gazed tenderly upon the upturned, smiling face, and then, pushing back the black tresses, he touched her white forehead with his lips.

Arthur Wayne was looking out from his lattice above, and his eye chanced to turn that way at the moment of the meeting. He started as if struck with a sudden pang, and his cheek, always pale, became of an ashen hue. Long he gazed with labored breath upon the pair, as if unable to realize what he had seen; then, with a suppressed moan, he sank into a chair, and leaned his brow heavily upon his hand. Thus for half an hour he remained motionless; it was only after a second summons that he roused himself and descended to the morning meal.

At the breakfast table Oriana was in high spirits, and failed to observe that Arthur was more sad than usual. Her brother, however, was preoccupied and thoughtful, and even Harold, although happy in the society of one he loved, could not refrain from moments of abstraction. Of course the adventure of the preceding night was concealed from Oriana, but it yet furnished the young men with matter for reflection; and, coupled with the exciting intelligence from South Carolina, it suggested, to Harold especially, a vision of an unhappy future. It was natural that the thought should obtrude itself of how soon a barrier might be placed between friends and loved ones, and the most sacred ties sundered, perhaps forever.

Miss Randolph, Oriana's aunt, usually reserved and silent, seemed on this occasion the most inquisitive and talkative of the party. Her interest in the momentous turn that affairs had taken was naturally aroused, and she questioned the young men closely as to their view of the probable consequences.

"Surely," she remarked, "a nation of Christian people will choose some alternative other than the sword to adjust their differences."

"Why, aunt," replied Oriana, with spirit, "what better weapon than the sword for the oppressed?"

"I fear there is treason lurking in that little heart of yours," said Harold, with a pensive smile.

"I am a true Southerner, Mr. Hare; and if

I were a man, I would take down my father's rifle and march into General Beauregard's camp. We have been too long anathematized as the vilest of God's creatures, because we will not turn over to the world's cold charity the helpless beings that were bequeathed into our charge by our fathers. I would protect my slave against Northern fanaticism as firmly as I would guard my children from the interference of a stranger, were I a mother."

"The government against which you would rebel," said Harold, "contemplates no interference with your slaves."

"Why, Mr. Hare," rejoined Oriana, warmly, "we of the South can see the spirit of abolitionism sitting in the executive chair, as plainly as we see the sunshine on an unclouded summer day. As well might we change places with our bondmen, as submit to this deliberate crusade against our institutions. Mr. Wayne, you are a man not prone to prejudice, I sincerely believe. Would you from your heart assert that this government is not hostile to Southern slavery?"

"I believe you are, on both sides, too sensitive upon the unhappy subject. You are breeding danger, and perhaps ruin, out of abstract ideas, and civil war will have laid the country waste before either party will have awakened to a knowledge that no actual cause of contention exists."

"Perhaps," said Beverly, "the mere fact that the two sections are hostile in sentiment, is the best reason why they should be hostile in deed, if a separation can only be accomplished by force of arms."

"And do you really fancy," said Harold, sharply, "that a separation is possible, in the face of the opposition of twenty millions of loyal citizens?"

"Yes," interrupted Oriana, "in the face of the opposing world. We established our right to self-government in 1776; and in 1861 we are prepared to prove our power to sustain that right."

"You are a young enthusiast," said Harold, smiling. "This rebellion will be crushed before the flowers in that garden shall be touched with the earliest frost."

"I think you have formed a false estimate of the movement," remarked Beverly, gravely;

"or rather, you have not fully considered of the subject."

"Harold," said Arthur, sadly, "I regret, and perhaps censure, equally with yourself, the precipitancy of our Carolinian brothers; but this is not an age, nor a country, where six millions of freeborn people can be controlled by bayonets and cannon."

They were about rising from the table, when a servant announced that some gentlemen desired to speak with Mr. Weems in private. He passed into the drawing-room, and found himself in the presence of three men, two of whom he recognized as small farmers of the neighborhood, and the other as the landlord of a public house. With a brief salutation, he seated himself beside them, and after a few commonplace remarks, paused, as if to learn their business with him.

After a little somewhat awkward hesitation, the publican broke silence.

"Squire Weems, we've called about a rather unpleasant sort of business"——

"The sooner we transact it, then, the better for all, I fancy, gentlemen."

"Just so. Old Judge Weems, your father, was a true Virginian, squire, and we know you are of the right sort, too." Beverly bowed in acknowledgment of the compliment. "Squire, the boys hereabouts met down thar at my house last night, to take into consideration them two Northern fellows that are putting up with you."

"Well, sir?"

"We don't want any Yankee abolitionists in these parts."

"Mr. Lucas, I have no guests for whom I will not vouch."

"Can't help that, squire, them chaps is spotted, and the boys have voted they must leave. As they be your company, us three've been deputized to call on you and have a talk about it. We don't want to do nothing unpleasant whar you're consarned, squire."

"Gentlemen, my guests shall remain with me while they please to honor me with their company, and I will protect them from violence or indignity with my life."

"There's no mistake but you're good grit, squire, but 'tain't no use. You know what the boys mean to do, they'll do. Now, whar's the good of kicking up a shindy about it?"

"No good whatever, Mr. Lucas. You had better let this matter drop. You know me too well to suppose that I would harbor dangerous characters. It is my earnest desire to avoid everything that may bring about an unnecessary excitement, or disturb the peace of the community; and I shall therefore make no secret of this intereviw to my friends. But whether they remain with me or go, shall be entirely at their option. I trust that my roof will be held sacred by my fellow-citizens."

"There'll be no harm done to you or yours, Squire Weems, whatever happens. But those strangers had better be out of these parts by to-morrow, sure. Good morning, squire."

"Good morning, gentlemen."

And the three worthies took their departure, not fully satisfied whether the object of their mission had been fulfilled.

Beverly, anxious to avoid a collision with the wild spirits of the neighborhood, which would be disagreeable, if not dangerous, to his guests, frankly related to Harold and Arthur the tenor of the conversation that had passed. Oriana was on fire with indignation, but her concern for Harold's safety had its weight with her, and she wisely refrained from opposing their departure; and both the young men, aware that a prolongation of their visit would cause the family at Riverside manor much inconvenience and anxiety, straightway announced their intention of proceeding northward on the following morning.

But it was no part of Seth Rawbon's purpose to allow his rival, Hare, to depart in peace. The chastisement which he had received at Harold's hands added a most deadly hate to the jealousy which his knowledge of Oriana's preference had caused. He had considerable influence with several of the dissolute and lawless characters of the vicinity, and a liberal allowance of Monongahela, together with sundry pecuniary favors, enabled him to depend upon their assistance in any adventure that did not promise particularly serious results. Now the capture and mock trial of a couple of Yankee strangers did not seem much out of the way to these not over-scrupulous worthies; and Rawbon's cunning representations as to the extent of their abolition proclivities were scarcely necessary, in view of the liberality of his bribes, to secure their coöperation in his scheme.

Rawbon had been prowling about the manor house during the day, in the hope of obtaining some clue to the intentions of the inmates, and observing a mulatto boy engaged in arranging the boat for present use, he walked carelessly along the bank to the old boat-house, and, by a few adroit questions, ascertained that "Missis and the two gen'lmen gwine to take a sail this arternoon."

The evening was drawing on apace when Oriana, accompanied by Arthur and Harold, set forth on the last of the many excursions they had enjoyed on James River; but they had purposely selected a late hour, that on their return they might realize the tranquil pleasures of a sail by moonlight. Beverly was busy finishing some correspondence for the North, which he intended giving into the charge of his friend Arthur, and he therefore remained at home. Phil, a smart mulatto, about ten years of age, who was a general favorite in the family and an especial pet of Oriana, was allowed to accompany the party.

It was a lovely evening, only cool enough to be comfortable for Oriana to be wrapped in her woollen shawl. As the shadows of twilight darkened on the silent river, a spirit of sadness was with the party, that vague and painful melancholy that weighs upon the heart when happy ties are about to be sundered, and loved ones are about to part. Arthur had brought his flute, and with an effort to throw off the feeling of gloom, he essayed a lively air; but it seemed like discord by association with their thoughts. He ceased abruptly, and, at Oriana's request, chose a more mournful theme. When the last notes of the plaintive melody had been lost in the stillness of the night, there was an oppressive pause, only broken by the rustle of the little sail and the faint rippling of the wave.

"I seem to be sailing into the shadows of misfortune," said Oriana, in a low, sad tone. "I wish the moon would rise, for this darkness presses upon my heart like the fingers of a sorrowful destiny. What a coward I am to-night!"

"A most obedient satellite," replied Arthur.

"Look where she heralds her approach by spreading a misty glow on the brow of yonder hill."

"We have left the shadows of misfortune behind us," said Harold, as a flood of moonlight flashed over the river, seeming to dash a million of diamonds in the path of the gliding boat.

"Alas! the fickle orb!" murmured Oriana; "it rises but to mock us, and hides itself already in the bosom of that sable cloud. Is there not a threat of rain there, Mr. Hare?"

"It looks unpromising, at the best," said Harold; "I think it would be prudent to return."

Suddenly, little Phil, who had been lying at ease, with his head against the thwarts, arose on his elbow and cried out:

"Wha' dat?"

"What is what, Phil?" asked Oriana. "Why, Phil, you have been dreaming," she added, observing the lad's confusion at having spoken so vehemently.

"Miss Orany, dar's a boat out yonder. I heard 'em pulling, sure."

"Nonsense, Phil! you've been asleep."

"By Gol! I heard 'em, sure. What a boat doing round here dis time o' night? Dem's some niggers arter chickens, sure."

And little Phil, satisfied that he had fathomed the mystery, lay down again in a fit of silent indignation. The boat was put about, but the wind had died away, and the sail flapped idly against the mast. Harold, glad of the opportunity for a little exercise, shipped the sculls and bent to his work.

"Miss Oriana, put her head for the bank if you please. We shall have less current to pull against in-shore."

The boat glided along under the shadow of the bank, and no sound was heard but the regular thugging and splashing of the oars and the voices of insects on the shore. They approached a curve in the river where the bank was thickly wooded, and dense shrubbery projected over the stream.

"Wha' dat?" shouted Phil again, starting up in the bow and peering into the darkness. A boat shot out from the shadow of the foliage, and her course was checked directly in their path. The movement was so sudden that, before

Harold could check his headway, the two boats fouled. A boathook was thrust into the thwarts; Arthur sprang to the bows to cast it off.

"Don't touch that," shouted a hoarse voice; and he felt the muzzle of a pistol thrust into his breast.

"None of that, Seth," cried another; and the speaker laid hold of his comrade's arm. "We must have no shooting, you know."

Arthur had thrown off the boathook, but some half-dozen armed men had already leaped into the frail vessel, crowding it to such an extent that a struggle, even had it not been madness against such odds, would have occasioned great personal danger to Oriana. Both Arthur and Harold seemed instinctively to comprehend this, and therefore offered no opposition. Their boat was taken in tow, and in a few moments the entire party, with one exception, were landed upon the adjacent bank. That exception was little Phil. In the confusion that ensued upon the collision of the two boats, the lad had quietly slipped overboard, and swam around to the stern where his mistress sat.

"Miss Orany, hist! Miss Orany!"

The bewildered girl turned and beheld the black face peering over the gunwale.

"Miss Orany, here I is. O Lor'! Miss Orany, what we gwine to do?"

She bowed her head toward him and whispered hurriedly, but calmly:

"Mind what I tell you, Phil. You watch where they take us to, and then run home and tell Master Beverly. Do you understand me, Phil?"

"Yes, I does, Miss Orany;" and the little fellow struck out silently for the shore, and crept among the bushes.

Oriana betrayed no sign of fear as she stood with her two companions on the bank a few paces from their captors. The latter, in a low but earnest tone, were disputing with one who seemed to act as their leader.

"You didn't tell us nothing about the lady," said a brawny, rugged-looking fellow, angrily. "Now, look here, Seth Rawbon, this ain't a goin' to do. I'd cut your heart out, before I'd let any harm come to Squire Weems' sister."

"You lied to us, you long-headed Yankee

turncoat," muttered another. What in thunder do you mean bringing us down here for kidnapping a lady?"

"Ain't I worried about it as much as you?" answered Rawbon. "Can't you understand it's all a mistake?"

"Well, now, you go and apologize to Miss Weems and fix matters, d'ye hear?"

"But what can we do?"

"Do? Undo what you've done, and show her back into the boat."

"But the two abo"——

"Damn them and you along with 'em! Come, boys, don't let's keep the lady waiting thar."

The party approached their prisoners, and one among them, hat in hand, respectfully addressed Oriana.

"Miss Weems, we're plaguy sorry this should 'a happened. It's a mistake and none of our fault. Your boat's down thar and yer shan't be merlested."

"Am I free to go?" asked Oriana, calmly.

"Free as air, Miss Weems."

"With my companions?"

"No, they remain with us," said Rawbon.

"Then I remain with them," she replied, with dignity and firmness.

The man who had first remonstrated with Rawbon, stepped up to him and laid his hand heavily on his shoulder:

"Look here, Seth Rawbon, you've played out your hand in this game, now mind that. Miss Weems, you're free to go, anyhow, with them chaps or not, just as you like."

"They stepped down the embankment, but the boats were nowhere to be seen. Rawbon, anticipating some trouble with his gang, had made a pretence only of securing the craft to a neighboring bush. The current had carried the boats out into the stream, and they had floated down the river and were lost to sight in the darkness.

CHAPTER V.

There was no remedy but to cross the woodland and cornfields that for about a league intervened between their position and the highway. They commenced the tedious tramp, Arthur and Harold exerting themselves to the utmost to protect Oriana from the brambles, and to guide her footsteps along the uneven ground and among the decayed branches and other obstacles that beset their path. Their rude companions, too, with the exception of Rawbon, who walked moodily apart, seemed solicitous to assist her with their rough attentions. To add to the disagreeable nature of their situation, the rain began to fall in torrents before they had accomplished one half of the distance. They were then in the midst of a tract of wooded land that was almost impassable for a lady in the darkness, on account of the yielding nature of the soil, and the numerous ruts and hollows that were soon transformed into miniature pools and streams. Oriana strove to treat the adventure as a theme for laughter, and for awhile chatted gaily with her companions; but it was evident that she was fast becoming weary, and that her thin-shod feet were wounded by constant contact with the twigs and sharp stones that it was impossible to avoid in the darkness. Her dress was torn, and heavy with mud and moisture, and the two young men were pained to perceive that, in spite of her efforts and their watchful care, she stumbled frequently with exhaustion, and leaned heavily on their arms as she labored through the miry soil.

One of the party opportunely remembered a charcoal-burner's hut in the vicinity, that would at least afford a rude shelter from the driving storm. Several of the men hastened in search of it, and soon a halloo not far distant indicated that the cabin, such as it was, had been discovered. As they approached, they were surprised to observe rays of light streaming through the cracks and crevices, as if a fire were blazing within. It was an uninviting structure, hastily constructed of unhewn logs, and upon ordinary occasions Oriana would have hesitated to pass the threshold; but wet and weary as she was, she was glad to obtain the shelter of even so poor a hovel.

"There's a runaway in thar, I reckon," said one of the party. He threw open the door, and several of the men entered. A fire of logs was burning on the earthen floor, and beside it was stretched a negro's form, wrapped in a tattered blanket. He started up as his unwelcome visitors entered, and looked frightened and bewildered, as if suddenly awakened from a sound sleep. However, he had no sooner laid eyes upon Seth Rawbon than, with a yell of fear, he sprang with a powerful leap through the doorway, leaving his blanket in the hands of those who sought to grasp him.

"That's my nigger Jim!" cried Rawbon, discharging his revolver at the dusky form as it ran like a deer into the shadow of the woods. At every shot, the negro jumped and screamed, but, from his accelerated speed, was apparently untouched.

"After him, boys!" shouted Rawbon. "Five dollars apiece and a gallon of whisky if you bring the varmint in."

With a whoop, the whole party went off in chase and were soon lost to view in the darkness.

Harold and Arthur led Oriana into the hut, and, spreading their coats upon the damp floor, made a rude couch for her beside the fire. The poor girl was evidently prostrated with fatigue and excitement, yet, with a faint laugh and a jest as she glanced around upon the questionable accommodations, she thanked them for their kindness, and seated herself beside the blazing fagots.

"This is a strange finale to our pleasure excursion," she said, as the grateful warmth somewhat revived her spirits. "You must acknowledge me a prophetess, gentlemen," she added, with a smile, "for you see that we sailed indeed into the shadows of misfortune."

"Should your health not suffer from this exposure," replied Arthur, "our adventure will prove no misfortune, but only a theme for mirth hereafter, when we recall to mind our present piteous plight."

"Oh, I am strong, Mr. Wayne," she answered cheerfully, perceiving the expression of solicitude in the countenances of her companions, "and have passed the ordeal of many a thorough wetting with impunity. Never fear but I shall fare well enough. I am only sorry and ashamed that all our boasted Virginia hospitality can afford you no better quarters than this for your last night among us."

"Apart from the discomfort to yourself, this little episode will only make brighter by contrast my remembrance of the many happy hours we have passed together," said Arthur, with a tone of deep feeling that caused Oriana to turn and gaze thoughtfully into the flaming pile.

Harold said nothing, and stood leaning moodily against the wall of the hovel, evidently a prey to painful thoughts. His mind wandered into the glooms of the future, and dwelt upon the hour when he, perhaps, should tread with hostile arms the soil that was the birthplace of his beloved. "Can it be possible," he thought, "that between us twain, united as we are in soul, there can exist such variance of opinion as will make her kin and mine enemies, and perhaps the shedders of each other's blood!"

There was a pause, and Oriana, her raiment

being partially dried, rested her head upon her arm and slumbered.

The storm increased in violence, and the rain, pelting against the cabin roof, with its weird music, formed a dismal accompaniment to the grotesque discomfort of their situation. Arthur threw fresh fuel upon the fire, and the crackling twigs sent up a fitful flame, that fell athwart the face of the sleeping girl, and revealed an expression of sorrow upon her features that caused him to turn away with a sigh.

"Arthur," asked Harold, abruptly, "do you think this unfortunate affair at Sumter will breed much trouble?"

"I fear it," said Arthur, sadly. "Our Northern hearts are made of sterner stuff than is consistent with the spirit of conciliation."

"And what of Southern hearts?"

"You have studied them," said Arthur, with a pensive smile, and bending his gaze upon the sleeping maiden.

Harold colored slightly, and glanced half reproachfully at his friend.

"I cannot help believing," continued the latter, "that we are blindly invoking a fatal strife.

more in the spirit of exaltation than of calm and searching philosophy. I am confident that the elements of union still exist within the sections, but my instinct, no less than my judgment, tells me that they will no longer exist when the chariot-wheels of war shall have swept over the land. Whatever be the disparity of strength, wealth and numbers, and whatever may be the result of encounters upon the battle-field, such a terrible war as both sides are capable of waging can never build up or sustain a fabric whose cement must be brotherhood and kindly feeling. I would as soon think to woo the woman of my choice with angry words and blows, as to reconcile our divided fellow citizens by force of arms."

"You are more a philosopher than a patriot," said Harold, with some bitterness.

"Not so," answered Arthur, warmly. "I love my country—so well, indeed, that I cannot be aroused into hostility to any section of it. My reason does not admit the necessity for civil war, and it becomes therefore a sacred obligation with me to give my voice against the doctrine of coercion. My judgment may err, or my sensibilities may be 'too full of the milk of human kindness' to serve the stern exigencies of the crisis with a Spartan's callousness and a Roman's impenetrability; but for you to affirm that, because true to my own opinions, I must be false to my country, is to deny me that independence of thought to which my country, as a nation, owes its existence and its grandeur."

"You boast your patriotism, and yet you seem to excuse those who seek the dismemberment of your country."

"I do not excuse them, but I would not have them judged harshly, for I believe they have acted under provocation."

"What provocation can justify rebellion against a government so beneficent as ours?"

"I will not pretend to justify, because I think there is much to be forgiven on either side. But if anything can palliate the act, it is that system of determined hostility which for years has been levelled against an institution which they believe to be righteous and founded upon divine precept. But I think this is not the hour for justification or for crimination. I am convinced that the integrity of the Union can only be preserved by withholding the armed hand at this crisis. And pray Heaven, our government may forbear to strike!"

"Would you, then, have our flag trampled upon with impunity, and our government confessed a cipher, because, forsooth, you have a constitutional repugnance to the severities of warfare? Away with such sickly sentimentality! Such theories, if carried into practice, would reduce us to a nation of political dwarfs and puny drivellers, fit only to grovel at the footstools of tyrants."

"I could better bear an insult to our flag than a deathblow to our nationality. And I feel that our nationality would not survive a struggle between the sections. There is no danger that we should be dwarfed in intellect or spirit by practising forbearance toward our brothers."

"Is treason less criminal because it is the treason of brother against brother? If so, then must a traitor of necessity go unpunished, since the nature of the crime requires that the culprit be your countryman. How hollow are your arguments when applied to existing facts!"

"You forget that I counsel moderation as an

expediency, as even a necessity, for the public good. It were poor policy to compass the country's ruin for the sake of bringing chastisement upon error."

"That can be but a questionable love of country that would humiliate a government to the act of parleying with rebellion."

"My love of country is not confined to one section of the country, or to one division of my countrymen. The lessons of the historic past have taught me otherwise. If, when a schoolboy, poring over the pages of my country's history, I have stood, in imagination, with Prescott at Bunker Hill, and stormed with Ethan Allen at the gates of Ticonderoga, I have also mourned with Washington at Valley Forge, and followed Marion and Sumter through the wilds of Carolina. If I have fancied myself at work with Yankee sailors at the guns, and poured the shivering broadside into the Guerriere, I have helped to man the breastworks at New Orleans, and seen the ranks that stood firm at Waterloo wavering before the blaze of Southern rifles. If I have read of the hardy Northern volunteers on the battle-plains of

Mexico; I remember the Palmetto boys at Cherubusco, and the brave Mississippians at Buena Vista. Is it a wonder, then, that my heartstrings ache when I see the links breaking that bind me to such memories? If I would have the Government parley awhile for the sake of peace, even although the strict law sanction the bayonet and cannon, I do it in the name of the sacred past, when the ties of brotherhood were strong. I counsel not humiliation nor submission, but conciliation. I counsel it, not only as an expedient, but as a tribute to the affinities of almost a century. I love the Union too well to be willing that its fate should be risked upon the uncertainties of war. I believe in my conscience that the chances of its reconstruction depend rather upon negotiation than upon battles. I may err, or you, as my opponent in opinion, may err; for while I assume not infallibility for myself, I deny it, with justice, to my neighbor. But I think as my heart and intellect dictate, and my patriotism should not be questioned by one as liable to error as myself. Should I yield my honest convictions upon a question of such vital importance as my country's welfare, then indeed should I be a traitor to my country and myself. But to accuse me of questionable patriotism for my independence of thought, is, in itself, treason against God and man."

"I believe you sincere in your convictions, Arthur, not because touched by your argument, but because I have known you too long and well to believe you capable of an unworthy motive. But what, in the name of common justice, would you have us do, when rebellion already thunders at the gates of our citadels with belching cannon? Shall we sit by our firesides and nod to the music of their artillery?"

"I would have every American citizen, in this crisis, as in all others, divest himself of all prejudice and sectional feeling: I would have him listen to and ponder upon the opinions of his fellow citizens, and, with the exercise of his best judgment, to discard the bad, and take counsel from the good; then, I would have him conclude for himself, not whether his flag has been insulted, or whether there are injuries to avenge, or criminals to be punished, but what is best and surest to be done for the welfare of his country. If he believe the Union can only be preserved by war, let his voice be for war; if by peace, let him counsel peace, as I do, from my heart; if he remain in doubt, let him incline to peace, secure that in so doing he will best obey the teachings of Christianity, the laws of humanity, and the mighty voice that is speaking from the soul of enlightenment, pointing out the errors of the past, and disclosing the secret of human happiness for the future."

Arthur's eye kindled as he spoke, and the flush of excitement, to which he was habitually a stranger, colored his pale cheek. Oriana had awakened with the vehemence of his language, and gazing with interest upon his now animated features, had been listening to his closing words. Harold was about to answer, when suddenly the baying of a hound broke through the noise of the storm.

"That is a bloodhound!" exclaimed Harold with an accent of surprise.

"Oh, no," said Oriana. "There are no bloodhounds in this neighborhood, nor are they at all in use, I am sure, in Virginia."

"I am not mistaken," replied Harold. "I have been made familiar with their baying while surveying on the coast of Florida. Listen!"

The deep, full tones came swelling upon the night wind, and fell with a startling distinctness upon the ear.

"It's my hound, Mister Hare," said a low, coarse voice at the doorway, and Seth Rawbon entered the cabin and closed the door behind him.

CHAPTER VI.

"It's my hound, Miss Weems, and I guess he's on the track of that nigger, Jim."

Oriana started as if stung by a serpent, and rising to her feet, looked upon the man with such an expression of contempt and loathing that the ruffian's brow grew black with anger as he returned her gaze. Harold confronted him, and spoke in a low, earnest tone, and between his clenched teeth:

"If you are a man you will go at once. This persecution of a woman is beneath even your brutality. If you have an account with me, I will not balk you. But relieve her from the outrage of your presence here."

"I guess I'd better be around," replied Rawbon, coolly, as he leaned against the door, with his hands in his coat pocket. "That dog is dangerous when he's on the scent. You see, Miss Weems," he continued, speaking over Harold's shoulder, "my niggers are plaguy troublesome, and I keep the hound to cow them down a trifle. But he wouldn't hurt a lady, I think—unless I happened to encourage him a bit, do you see."

And the man showed his black teeth with a grin that caused Oriana to shudder and turn away.

Harold's brow was like a thunder-cloud, from beneath which his eyes flashed like the lightning at midnight.

"Your words imply a threat which I cannot understand. Ruffian! What do mean?"

"I mean no good to you, my buck!"

His lip, with the deep cut upon it, curled with hate, but he still leaned coolly against the door, though a quick ear might have caught a click, as if he had cocked a pistol in his pocket. It was a habit with Harold to go unarmed. Fearless and self-reliant by nature, even upon his surveying expeditions in wild and out of the way districts, he carried no weapon beyond sometimes a stout oaken staff. But now, his form dilated, and the muscles of his arm contracted, as if he were about to strike. Oriana understood the movement and the danger. She advanced quietly but quickly to his side, and took his hand within her own.

"He is not worth your anger, Harold. For my sake, Harold, do not provoke him further," she added softly, as she drew him from the spot.

At this moment the baying of the hound was heard, apparently in close proximity to the hovel, and presently there was a heavy breathing and snuffling at the threshold, followed by a bound against the door, and a howl of rage and impatience. Nothing prevented the entrance of the animal except the form of Rawbon, who still leaned quietly against the rude frame, which, hanging upon leathern hinges, closed the aperture.

There was something frightful in the hoarse snarling of the angry beast, as he dashed his his heavy shoulder against the rickety framework, and Oriana shrank nervously to Harold's side.

"Secure that dog!" he said, as, while soothing the trembling girl, he looked over his shoulder reproachfully at Rawbon. His tone was low, and even gentle, but it was tremulous with passion. But the man gave no answer, and continued leering at them as before.

Arthur walked to him and spoke almost in an accent of entreaty.

"Sir, for the sake of your manhood, take away your dog and leave us."

He did not answer.

The hound, excited by the sound of voices, redoubled his efforts and his fury. Oriana was sinking into Harold's arms.

"This must end," he muttered. "Arthur, take her from me, she's fainting. I'll go out and brain the dog."

"Not yet, not yet," whispered Arthur. "For her sake be calm," and while he received Oriana upon one arm, with the other he sought to stay his friend.

But Harold seized a brand from the fire, and sprang toward the door.

"Stand from the door," he shouted, lifting the brand above Rawbon's head. "Leave that, I say!"

Rawbon's lank form straightened, and in an instant the revolver flashed in the glare of the fagots.

He did not shoot, but his face grew black with passion.

"By God! you strike me, and I'll set the dog at the woman."

At the sound of his master's voice, the hound set up a yell that seemed unearthly. Harold was familiar with the nature of the species, and even in the extremity of his anger, his anxiety for Oriana withheld his arm.

"Look you here!" continued Rawbon, losing his quiet, mocking tone, and fairly screaming with excitement, "do you see this?" He pointed to his mangled lip, from which, by the action of his jaws while talking, the plaster had just been torn, and the blood was streaming out afresh. "Do you see this? I've got that to settle with you. I'll hunt you, by G—d! as that hound hunts a nigger. Now see if I don't spoil that pretty face of yours, some day, so that she won't look so sweet on you for all your pretty talk."

He seemed to calm abruptly after this, put up his pistol, and resumed the wicked leer.

"What would you have?" at last asked Arthur, mildly and with no trace of anger in his voice.

Rawbon turned to him with a searching glance, and, after a pause, said:

"Terms."

"What?"

"I want to make terms with you."

"About what?"

"About this whole affair."

"Well. Go on."

"I know you can hurt me for this with the law, and I know you mean to. Now I want this matter hushed up."

Harold would have spoken, but Arthur implored him with a glance, and answered:

"What assurance can you give us against your outrages in the future?"

"None."

"None! Then why should we compromise with you?"

"Because I've got the best hand to-night, and you know it. For her, you know, you'll do 'most anything—now, won't you?"

The fellow's complaisant smile caused Arthur to look away with disgust. He turned to Harold, and they were conferring about Rawbon's strange proposition, when Oriana raised her head suddenly and her face assumed an expression of attention, as if her ear had caught a distant sound. She had not forgotten little Phil, and knowing his sagacity and faithfulness, she depended much upon his having followed her instructions. And indeed, a moment after, the plashing of the hoofs of horses in the wet soil could be distinctly heard.

"Them's my overseer and his man, I guess," said Rawbon, with composure, and he smiled again as he observed how effectually he had checked the gleam of joy that had lightened Oriana's face.

"'Twas he, you see, that set the dog on Jim's track, and now he's following after, that's all."

He had scarcely concluded, when a vigorous and excited voice was heard, shouting: "There 'tis!—there's the hut, gentlemen! Push on!"

"It is my brother! my brother!" cried Oriana, clasping her hands with joy; and for the first time that night she burst into tears and sobbed on Harold's shoulder.

Rawbon's face grew livid with rage and disappointment. He flung open the door and sprang out into the open air; but Oriana could see him pause an instant at the threshold, and stooping, point into the cabin. The low hissing word of command that accompanied the action reached her ear. She knew what it meant and a faint shriek burst from her lips, more perhaps from horror at the demoniac cruelty of the man, than from fear. The next moment, a gigantic bloodhound, gaunt, mud-bespattered and with the froth of fury oozing from his distended jaws, plunged through the doorway and stood glaring in the centre of the cabin.

Oriana stood like a sculptured ideal of terror, white and immovable; Harold with his left arm encircled the rigid form, while his right hand was uplifted, weaponless, but clenched with the energy of despair, till the blood-drops burst from his palm. But Arthur stepped before them both and fixed his calm blue eyes upon the monster's burning orbs. There was neither fear, nor excitement, nor irresolution in that steadfast gaze—it was like the clear, straightforward glance of a father checking a wayward child—even the habitual sadness lingered in the deep azure, and the features only changed to be cast in more placid mold. It was the struggle of a brave and tranquil soul with the ferocious instincts of the brute. The hound, crouched for a deadly spring, was fascinated by this spectacle of the utter absence of emotion. His huge chest heaved like a billow with his labored respiration, but the regular breathing of the being that awed him was like that of a sleeping child. For full five minutes—but it seemed an age—this silent but terrible duel was being fought, and yet no succor came. Beverly and those who came with him must have changed their course to pursue the fleeing Rawbon.

"Lead her out softly, Harold," murmured Arthur, without changing a muscle or altering his gaze. But the agony of suspense had been too great—Oriana, with a convulsive shudder, swooned and hung like a corpse upon Harold's arm.

"Oh, God! she is dying, Arthur!" he could not help exclaiming, for it was indeed a counterpart of death that he held in his embrace.

Then only did Arthur falter for an instant, and the hound was at his throat. The powerful jaws closed with a snap upon his shoulder, and you might have heard the sharp fangs grate against the bone. The shock of the spring brought Arthur to the ground, and man and brute rolled over together, and struggled in the mud and gore. Harold bore the lifeless girl out into the air, and returning, closed the door. He seized a brand, and with both hands levelled a fierce blow at the dog's neck. The stick shivered like glass, but the creature only shook his grisly head, but never quit his hold. With his bare hand he seized the live coals from the thickest of the fire and pressed them against the flanks and stomach of the tenacious animal; the brute howled and quivered in every limb, but still the blood-stained fangs were firmly set into the lacerated flesh. With both hands clasped around the monster's throat, he exerted his strength till the finger-bones seemed to crack. He could feel the pulsations of the dog's heart grow fainter and slower, and could see in his rolling and upheaved eyeballs that the death-pang was upon him; but those iron jaws still were locked in the torn shoulder; and as Harold beheld the big drops start from his friend's ashy brow, and his eyes filming with the leaden hue of unconsciousness, the agonizing thought came to him that the dog and the man were dying together in that terrible embrace.

It was then that he fairly sobbed with the sensation of relief, as he heard the prancing of steeds close by the cabin-door; and Beverly, entering hastily, with a cry of horror, stood one moment aghast as he looked on the frightful scene. Then, with repeated shots from his revolver, he scattered the dog's brains over Arthur's blood-stained bosom.

Harold arose, and, faint and trembling with excitement and exhaustion, leaned against the wall. Beverly knelt by the side of the wounded man, and placed his hand above his heart. Harold turned to him with an anxious look.

"He has but fainted from loss of blood," said Beverly. "Harold, where is my sister?"

As he spoke, Oriana, who, in the fresh night air, had recovered from her swoon, pale and with dishevelled hair, appeared at the cabin-door. Harold and Beverly sought to lead her out before her eyes fell upon Arthur's bleeding form; but she had already seen the pale, calm face, clotted with blood, but with the beautiful sad smile still lingering upon the parted lips. She appeared to see neither Harold nor her brother, but only those tranquil features, above which the angel of Death seemed already to have brushed his dewy wing. She put aside Beverly's arm, which was extended to support her, and thrust him away as if he had been a stranger. She unloosed her hand from Harold's affectionate grasp, and with a long and suppressed moan of intense anguish, she kneeled down in the little pool of blood beside the extended form, with her hands tightly clasped, and wept bitterly.

They raised her tenderly, and assured her that Arthur was not dead.

"Oh, no! oh, no!" she murmured, as the tears streamed out afresh, "he must not die! He must not die for *me!* He is so good! so brave! A child's heart, with the courage of a lion. Oh, Harold! why did you not save him?"

But as she took Harold's hand almost reproachfully, she perceived that it was black and burnt, and he too was suffering; and she leaned her brow upon his bosom and sobbed with a new sorrow.

Beverly was almost vexed at the weakness his sister displayed. It was unusual to her, and he forgot her weariness and the trial she had passed. He had been binding some linen about Arthur's shoulder, and he looked up and spoke to her in a less gentle tone.

"Oriana, you are a child to-night. I have never seen you thus. Come, help me with this bandage."

She sighed heavily, but immediately ceased to weep, and said "Yes," calmly and with firmness. Bending beside her brother, without faltering or shrinking, she gave her white fingers to the painful task.

In the stormy midnight, by the fitful glare of the dying embers, those two silent men and that pale woman seemed to be keeping a vigil in an abode of death. And the pattering rain and moan of the night-wind sounded like a dirge.

CHAPTER VII.

Several gentlemen of the neighborhood, whom Beverly, upon hearing little Phil's story, had hastily summoned to his assistance, now entered the cabin, together with the male negroes of his household, who had mounted the farm horses and eagerly followed to the rescue of their young mistress. They had been detained without by an unsuccessful pursuit of Rawbon, whose flight they had discovered, but who had easily evaded them in the darkness. A rude litter was constructed for Arthur, but Oriana declared herself well able to proceed on horseback, and would not listen to any suggestion of delay on her account. She mounted Beverly's horse, while he and Harold supplied themselves from among the horses that the negroes had rode, and thus, slowly and silently, they threaded the lonely forest, while ever and anon a groan from the litter struck painfully upon their ears.

4*

Arrived at the manor house, a physician who had been summoned, pronounced Arthur's hurt to be serious, but not dangerous. Upon receiving this intelligence, Oriana and Harold were persuaded to retire, and Beverly and his aunt remained as watchers at the bedside of the wounded man.

Oriana, despite her agitation, slept well, her rest being only disturbed by fitful dreams, in which Arthur's pale face seemed ever present, now smiling upon her mournfully, and now locked in the repose of death. She arose somewhat refreshed, though still feverish and anxious, and walking upon the veranda to breathe the morning air, she was joined by Harold, with his hand in a sling, and much relieved by the application of a poultice, which the skill of Miss Randolph had prepared. He informed her that Arthur was sleeping quietly, and that she might dismiss all fears as to his safety; and perhaps, if he had watched her closely, the earnest expression of something more than pleasure with which she received this assurance, might have given him cause for rumination. Beverly descended soon afterward, and confirmed the favorable report from the sick chamber, and Oriana retired into the house to assist in preparing the morning meal.

"Let us take a stroll by the riverside," said Beverly; "the air breathes freshly after my night's vigil."

"The storm has left none but traces of beauty behind," observed Harold, as they crossed the lawn. The loveliness of the early morning was indeed a pleasant sequel to the rude tempest of the preceding night. The dewdrops glistened upon grass-blade and foliage, and the bosom of the stream flashed merrily in the sunbeams.

"It is," answered Beverly, "as if Nature were rejoicing that the war of the elements is over, and a peace proclaimed. Would that the black cloud upon our political horizon had as happily passed away."

After a pause, he continued: "Harold, you need not fear to remain with us a while longer. I am sure that Rawbon's confederates are heartily ashamed of their participation in last night's outrage, and will on no account be seduced to a similar adventure. Rawbon himself will not be likely to show himself in this vicinity for some time to come, unless as the inmate of a jail, for I have ordered a warrant to be issued against him. The whole affair has resulted evidently from some unaccountable antipathy which the fellow entertains against us."

"I agree with you," replied Harold, "but still I think this is an unpropitious time for the prolongation of my visit. There are events, I fear, breeding for the immediate future, in which I must take a part. I shall only remain with you a few days, that I may be assured of Arthur's safety."

"I will not disguise from you my impression that Virginia will withdraw from the Union. In that case, we will be nominal enemies. God grant that our paths may not cross each other."

"Amen!" replied Harold, with much feeling. "But I do not understand why we should be enemies. You surely will not lend your voice to this rebellion?"

"When the question of secession is before the people of my State, I shall cast my vote as my judgment and conscience shall dictate. Meanwhile I shall examine the issue, and, I trust, dispassionately. But whatever may become of my individual opinion, where Virginia goes I go, whatever be the event."

"Would you uphold a wrong in the face of your own conscience?"

"Oh, as to that, I do not hold it a question between right and wrong, but simply of advisability. The right of secession I entertain no doubt about."

"No doubt as to the right of dismembering and destroying a government which has fostered your infancy, developed your strength, and made you one among the parts of a nation that has no peer in a world's history? Is it possible that intellect and honesty can harbor such a doctrine!"

"My dear Harold, you look at the subject as an enthusiast, and you allow your heart not to assist but to control your brain. Men, by association, become attached to forms and symbols, so as in time to believe that upon their existence depends the substance of which they are but the signs. Forty years ago, in the Hawaiian Islands, the death-penalty was inflicted upon a native of the inferior caste, should he chance to pass over the shadow of one of noble birth So would you avenge an insult to a shadow, while you allow the substance to be stolen from your grasp. Our jewel, as freemen, is the right of self-government; the form of government is a mere convenience—a machine, which may be dismembered, destroyed, remodelled a thousand times, without detriment to the great principle of which it is the outward sign."

"You draw a picture of anarchy that would disgrace a confederation of petty savage tribes. What miserable apology for a government would that be whose integrity depends upon the caprice of the governed?"

"It is as likely that a government should become tyrannical, as that a people should become capricious. You have simply chosen an unfair word. For *caprice* substitute *will*, and you have my ideal of a true republic."

"And by that ideal, one State, by its individual act, might overturn the entire system adopted for the convenience and safety of the whole."

"Not so. It does not follow that the system should be overturned because circumscribed in limit, more than that a business firm should necessarily be ruined by the withdrawal of a partner. Observe, Harold, that the General Government was never a sovereignty, and came into existence only by the consent of each and every individual State. The States were the sovereignties, and their connection with the Union, being the mere creature of their will, can exist only by that will."

"Why, Beverly, you might as well argue that this pencil-case, which became mine by an act of volition on your part, because you gave it me, ceases to be mine when you reclaim it."

"If I had appointed you my amanuensis, and had transferred my pencil to you simply for the purposes of your labor in my behalf, when I choose to dismiss you, I should expect the return of my property. The States made no gifts to the Federal Government for the sake of giving, but only delegated certain powers for specific purposes. They never could have delegated the power of coercion, since no one State or number of States possessed that power as against their sister States."

"But surely, in entering into the bonds of union, they formed a contract with each other which should be inviolable."

"Then, at the worst, the seceding States are guilty of a breach of contract with the remaining States, but not with the General Government, with which they made no contract. They formed a union, it is true. But of what? Of sovereignties. How can those States be sovereignties which admit a power above them, possessing the right of coercion? To admit the right of coercion is to deny the existence of sovereignity."

"You can find nothing in the Constitution to intimate the right of secession."

"Because its framers considered the right sufficiently established by the very nature of the confederation. The fears upon the subject that were expressed by Patrick Henry, and other zealous supporters of State Rights, were quieted by the assurances of the opposite party, who ridiculed the idea that a convention, similar to that which in each State adopted the Constitution, could not thereafter, in representation of the popular will, withdraw such

State from the confederacy. You have, in proof of this, but to refer to the annals of the occasion."

"I discard the theory as utterly inconsistent with any legislative power. We have either a government or we have not. If we have one, it must possess within itself the power to sustain itself. Our chief magistrate becomes otherwise a mere puppet, and our Congress a shallow mockery, and the shadow only of a legislative body. Our nationality becomes a word, and nothing more. Our place among the nations becomes vacant, and the great Republic, our pride and the world's wonder, crumbles into fragments, and with its downfall perishes the hope of the oppressed of every clime. I wonder, Beverly, that you can coldly argue against the very life of your country, and not feel the parricide's remorse! Have you no lingering affection for the glorious structure which our fathers built for and bequeathed to us, and which you now seek to hurl from its foundations? Have you no pride and love for the brave old flag that has been borne in the vanguard to victory so often, that has shrouded the lifeless form of Lawrence, that has gladdened the heart of the American wandering in foreign climes, and has spread its sacred folds over the head of Washington, here, on your own native soil?"

"Yes, Harold, yes! I love the Union, and I love and am proud of the brave old flag; I would die for either, and, although I reason with you coldly, my soul yearns to them both, and my heart aches when I think that soon, perhaps, they will no more belong to me. But I must sacrifice even my pride and love to a stern sense of duty. So Washington did, when he hurled his armed squadrons against the proud banner of St. George, under which he had been trained in soldiership, and had won the laurel of his early fame. He, too, no doubt, was not without a pang, to be sundered from his share of Old England's glorious memories, the land of his allegiance, the king whom he had served, the soil where the bones of his ancestors lay at rest. It would cause me many a throb of agony to draw my sword against the standard of the Republic—but I would do it, Harold, if my conscience bade me, although my nearest friends, although you, Harold—and I love you dearly—were in the foremost rank."

"Where I will strive to be, should my country call upon me. But Heaven forbid that we should meet thus, Beverly!"

"Heaven forbid?" he replied, with a sigh, as he pressed Harold's hand. "But yonder comes little Phil, running like mad, to tell us, doubtless, that breakfast is cold with waiting for us."

They retraced their steps, and found Miss Randolph and Oriana awaiting their presence at the breakfast-table.

CHAPTER VIII.

During the four succeeding days, the household at Riverside manor were much alarmed for Arthur's safety, for a violent fever had ensued, and, to judge from the physician's evasive answers, the event was doubtful. The family were unremitting in their attentions, and Oriana, quietly, but with her characteristic self-will, insisted upon fulfilling her share of the duties of a nurse. And no hand more gently smoothed the sick man's pillow or administered more tenderly the cooling draught. It seemed that Arthur's sleep was calmer when her form was bending over him, and even when his thoughts were wandering and his eyes were restless with delirium, they turned to welcome her as she took her accustomed seat. Once, while she watched there alone in the twilight, the open book unheeded in her hand, and her subdued eyes bent thoughtfully upon his face as he slept unconscious of her presence, she saw the white lips move and heard the murmur of the low, musical voice. Her fair head was bent to catch the words—they were the words of delirium or of dreams, but they brought a blush to her cheek. And yet she bent her head still lower and listened, until her forehead rested on the pillow, and when she looked up again with a sigh, and fixed her eyes mechanically on the page before her, there was a trace of tears upon the drooping lashes.

He awoke from a refreshing slumber and it seemed that the fever was gone; for his glance was calm and clear, and the old smile was upon his lips. When he beheld Oriana, a slight flush passed over his cheek.

"Are you indeed there, Miss Weems," he said, "or do I still dream? I have been dreaming, I know not what, but I was very happy." He sighed, and closed his eyes, as if he longed to woo back the vision which had fled. She seemed to know what he had been dreaming, for while his cheek paled again, hers glowed like an autumn cloud at sunset.

"I trust you are much better, Mr. Wayne?"

"Oh yes, much better. I fear I have been

very troublesome to you all. You have been very kind to me."

"Do not speak so, Mr. Wayne," she replied, and a tear glistened in her eyes. "If you knew how grateful we all are to you! You have suffered terribly for my sake, Mr. Wayne. You have a brave, pure heart, and I could hate myself with thinking that I once dared to wrong and to insult it."

"In my turn, I say do not speak so. I pray you, let there be no thoughts between us that make you unhappy. What you accuse yourself of, I have forgotten, or remember only as a passing cloud that lingered for a moment on a pure and lovely sky. There must be no self-reproaches between us twain, Miss Weems, for we must become strangers to each other in this world, and when we part I would not leave with you one bitter recollection."

There was sorrow in his tone, and the young girl paused awhile and gazed through the lattice earnestly into the gathering gloom of evening.

"We must not be strangers, Mr. Wayne."

"Alas! yes, for to be otherwise were fatal, at least to me."

She did not answer, and both remained silent and thoughtful, so long, indeed, that the night shadows obscured the room. Oriana arose and lit the lamp.

"I must go and prepare some supper for you," she said, in a lighter tone.

He took her hand as she stood at his bedside and spoke in a low but earnest voice:

"You must forget what I have said to you, Miss Weems. I am weak and feverish, and my brain has been wandering among misty dreams. If I have spoken indiscreetly, you will forgive me, will you not?"

"It is I that am to be forgiven, for allowing my patient to talk when the doctor prescribes silence. I am going to get your supper, for I am sure you must be hungry; so, good bye," she added gaily, as she smoothed the pillow, and glided from the room. Oriana was silent and reserved for some days after this, and Harold seemed also to be disturbed and ill at ease. Some link appeared to be broken between them, for she did not look into his eyes with the same frank, trusting gaze that had so often returned his glance of tenderness, and sometimes even she looked furtively away with heightened color, when, with some gentle commonplace, his voice broke in upon her meditation. Arthur was now able to sit for some hours daily in his easy-chair, and Oriana often came to him at such times, and although they conversed but rarely, and upon indifferent themes, she was never weary of reading to him, at his request, some favorite book. And sometimes, as the author's sentiment found an echo in her heart, she would pause and gaze listlessly at the willow branches that waved before the casement, and both would remain silent and pensive, till some member of the family entered, and broke in upon their revery.

"Come, Oriana," said Harold, one afternoon, "let us walk to the top of yonder hillock, and look at this glorious sunset."

She went for her bonnet and shawl, and joined him. They had reached the summit of the hill before either of them broke silence, and then Oriana mechanically made some commonplace remark about the beauty of the western sky. He replied with a monosyllable, and sat down upon a moss-covered rock. She plucked a few wild-flowers, and toyed with them.

"Oriana, Arthur is much better now."

"Much better, Harold."

"I have no fears for his safety now. I think I shall go to-morrow."

"Go, Harold?"

"Yes, to New York. The President has appealed to the States for troops. I am no soldier, but I cannot remain idle while my fellow citizens are rallying to arms."

"Will you fight, Harold?"

"If needs be."

"Against your countrymen?"

"Against traitors."

"Against me, perhaps."

"Heaven forbid that the blood of any of your kin should be upon my hands. I know how much you have suffered, dearest, with the thought that this unhappy business may separate us for a time. Think you that the eye of affection could fail to notice your dejection and reflective mood for some days past?"

Her face grew crimson, and she tore nervously the petals of the flower in her hand.

"Oriana, you are my betrothed, and no earthly discords should sever our destinies or estrange our hearts. Why should we part at all. Be mine at once, Oriana, and go with me to the loyal North, for none may tell how soon a barrier may be set between your home and me."

"That would be treason to my kindred and the home of my birth."

"And to be severed from me—would it not be treason to your heart?"

She did not answer.

"I have spoken to Beverly about it, and he will not seek to control you. We are most unhappy, Oriana, in our national troubles; why should we be so in our domestic ties. We can be blest, even among the rude alarms of war. This strife will soon be over, and you shall see the old homestead once again. But while the dark cloud lowers, I call upon you, in the name of your pledged affection, to share my fortunes with me, and bless me with this dear hand."

That hand remained passively within his own, but her bosom swelled with emotion, and presently the large tears rolled upon her cheek.

He would have pressed her to his bosom, but she gently turned from him, and sinking upon the sward, sobbed through her clasped fingers.

"Why are you thus unhappy, dear Oriana?" he murmured, as he bent tenderly above her. "Surely you do not love me less because of this poison of rebellion that infects the land. And with love, woman's best consolation, to be your comforter, why should you be unhappy?"

She arose, pale and excited, and raised his hand to her lips. The act seemed to him a strange one for an affianced bride, and he gazed upon her with a troubled air.

"Let us go home, Harold."

"But tell me that you love me."

She placed her two hands lightly about his neck, and looked up mournfully but steadily into his face.

"I will be your true wife, Harold, and pray heaven I may love you as you deserve to be loved. But I am not well to-day, Harold. Let us speak no more of this now, for there is something at my heart that must be quieted with penitence and prayer. Oh, do not question me, Harold," she added, as she leaned her cheek upon his breast; "we will talk with Beverly, and to-morrow I shall be stronger and less foolish. Come, Harold, let us go home."

She placed her arm within his, and they walked silently homeward. When they reached the house, Oriana was hastening to her chamber, but she lingered at the threshold, and returned to Harold.

"I am not well to-night, and shall not come down to tea. Good night, Harold. Smile upon me as you were wont to do," she added, as she pressed his hand and raised her swollen eyes, beneath whose white lids were crushed two tear-drops that were striving to burst forth. "Give me the smile of the old time, and the old kiss, Harold," and she raised her forehead to receive it. Do not look disturbed; I have but a headache, and shall be well to-morrow. Good night—dear—Harold."

She strove to look pleasantly as she left the room, but Harold was bewildered and anxious, and, till the summons came for supper, he paced the veranda with slow and meditative steps.

CHAPTER IX.

The following morning was warm and spring-like, and Arthur was sufficiently strong and well to walk out a little in the open air. He had been seated upon the veranda conversing with Beverly and Harold, when the latter proposed a stroll with Beverly, with whom he wished to converse in relation to his proposed marriage. As the beams of the unclouded sun had already chased away the morning dew, and the air was warm and balmy, Arthur walked out into the garden and breathed the freshness of the atmosphere with the exhilaration of a convalescent freed for the first time from the sick-room. Accidentally, or by instinct, he turned his steps to the little grove which he knew was Oriana's favorite haunt; and there, indeed, she sat, upon the rustic bench, above which the drooping limbs of the willow formed a leafy canopy. The pensive girl, her white hand, on which she leaned, buried among the raven tresses, was gazing fixedly into the depths of the clear sky, as if she sought to penetrate that azure veil, and find some hope realized among the mysteries of the space beyond. The neglected volume had fallen from her lap, and lay among the bluebells at her feet. Arthur's feeble steps were unheard upon the sward, and he had taken his seat beside her, before, conscious of an intruder, she started from her dream.

"The first pilgrimage of my convalescence is to your bower, my gentle nurse. I have come to thank you for more kindness than I can ever repay, except with grateful thoughts."

She had risen when she became aware of his presence; and when she resumed her seat, it seemed with hesitation, and almost an effort, as if two impulses were struggling within her. But her pleasure to see him abroad again was too hearty to be checked, and she timidly gave him the hand which his extended palm invited to a friendly grasp.

"Indeed, Mr. Wayne, I am very glad to see you so far recovered."

"To your kind offices chiefly I owe it, and those of my good friends, your brother and

Harold, and our excellent Miss Randolph. My sick-room has been the test of so much friendship, that I could almost be sinful enough to regret the returning health which makes me no longer a dependent on your care. But you are pale, Miss Weems. Or is it that my eyes are unused to this broad daylight? Indeed, I trust you are not ill?"

"Oh, no, I am quite well," she answered; but it was with an involuntary sigh that was in contrast with the words. "But you are not strong yet, Mr. Wayne, and I must not let you linger too long in the fresh morning air. We had best go in under shelter of the veranda."

She arose, and would have led the way, but he detained her gently with a light touch upon her sleeve.

"Stay one moment, I pray you. I seem to breathe new life with this pure air, and the perfume of these bowers awakens within me an inexpressible and calm delight. I shall be all the better for one tranquil hour with nature in bloom, if you, like the guardian nymph of these floral treasures, will sit beside me."

He drew her gently back into the seat, and

looked long and earnestly upon her face. She felt his gaze, but dared not return it, and her fair head drooped like a flower that bends beneath the glance of a scorching sun.

"Miss Weems," he said at last, but his voice was so low and tremulous that it scarce rose above the rustle of the swinging willow boughs, "you are soon to be a bride, and in your path the kind Destinies will shower blessings. When they wreathe the orange blossoms in your hair, and you are led to the altar by the hand to which you must cling for life, if I should not be there to wish you joy, you will not deem, will you, that I am less your friend?"

The fair head drooping yet lower was her only answer.

"And when you shall be the mistress of a home where Content will be shrined, the companion of your virtues, and over your threshold many friends shall be welcomed, if I should never sit beside your hearthstone, you will not, will you, believe that I have forgotten, or that I could forget?"

Still lower the fair head drooped, but she answered only with a falling tear.

"I told you the other day that we should be strangers through life, and why, I must not tell, although perhaps your woman's heart may whisper, and yet not condemn me for that which, Heaven knows, I have struggled against—alas, in vain! Do not turn from me. I would not breathe a word to you that in all honor you should not hear, although my heart seems bursting with its longing, and I would yield my soul with rapture from its frail casket, for but one moment's right to give its secret wings. I will bid you farewell to-morrow"——

"To-morrow!"

"Yes, the doctor says that the sea air will do me good, and an occasion offers to-morrow which I shall embrace. It will be like setting forth upon a journey through endless solitudes, where my only companions will be a memory and a sorrow."

He paused a while, but continued with an effort at composure.

"Our hearts are tyrants to us, Miss Weems, and will not, sometimes, be tutored into silence. I see that I have moved, but I trust not offended you."

"You have not offended," she murmured, but in so low a tone that perhaps the words were lost in the faint moan of the swaying foliage.

"What I have said," he continued earnestly, and taking her hand with a gentle but respectful pressure, "has been spoken as one who is dying speaks with his fleeting breath; for evermore my lips shall be shackled against my heart, and the past shall be sealed and avoided as a forbidden theme. We are, then, good friends at parting, are we not?"

"Yes."

"And, believe me, I shall be happiest when I think that you are happy—for you will be happy."

She sighed so deeply that the words were checked upon his lips, as if some new emotion had turned the current of his thought.

"Are you *not* happy?"

The tears that, in spite of her endeavor, burst from beneath the downcast lids, answered him as words could not have done. He was agitated and unnerved, and, leaning his brow against his hand, remained silent while she wept.

"Harold is a noble fellow," he said at last,

after a long silence, and when she had grown calmer, "and deserves to be loved as I am sure you love him."

"Oh, he has a noble heart, and I would die rather than cause him pain."

"And you love him ?"

"I thought I loved him."

The words were faint—hardly more than a breath upon her lips; but he heard them, and his heart grew big with an undefined awe, as if some vague danger were looming among the shadows of his destiny. Oriana turned to him suddenly, and clasped his hand within her trembling fingers.

"Oh, Mr. Wayne! you must go, and never see me more. I am standing on the brink of an abyss, and my heart bids me leap. I see the danger, and, oh God! I have prayed for power to shun it. But Arthur, Arthur, if you do not help me, I am lost. You are a man, an honest man, an honorable man, who will not wrong your friend, or tempt the woman that cannot love you without sin. Oh, save me from myself —from you—from the cruel wrong that I could even dream of against him to whom I have sworn my woman's faith. I am a child in your hands, Arthur, and in the face of the reproaching Providence above me, I feel—I feel that I am at your mercy. I feel that what you speak I must listen to; that should you bid me stand beside you at the altar, I should not have courage to refuse. I feel, oh God! Arthur, that I love you, and am betrothed to Harold. But you are strong—you have courage, will, the power to defy such weakness of the heart—and you will save me, for I know you are a good and honest man."

As she spoke, with her face upturned to him, and the hot tears rolling down her cheeks, her fingers convulsively clasped about his hand, and her form bending closer and closer toward him, till her cheek was resting on his bosom, Arthur shuddered with intensity of feeling, and from his averted eyes the scalding drops, that had never once before moistened their surface, betrayed how terribly he was shaken with emotion.

But while she spoke, rapt as they were within themselves, they saw not one who stood with folded arms beside the rustic bench, and gazed upon them.

"As God is my hope," said Arthur," I will

disarm temptation. Fear not. From this hour we part. Henceforth the living and the dead shall not be more estranged than we."

He arose, but started as if an apparition met his gaze. Oriana knelt beside him, and touched her lips to his hand in gratitude. An arm raised her tenderly, and a gentle voice murmured her name.

It was not Arthur's.

Oriana raised her head, with a faint cry of terror. She gasped and swooned upon the intruder's breast.

It was Harold Hare who held her in his arms.

Arthur, with folded arms, stood erect, but pale, in the presence of his friend. His eye, sorrowful, yet calm, was fixed upon Harold, as if awaiting his angry glance. But Harold looked only on the lifeless form he held, and parting the tresses from her cold brow, his lips rested there a moment with such a fond caress as sometimes a father gives his child.

"Poor girl!" he murmured, "would that my sorrow could avail for both. Arthur, I have heard enough to know you would not do me wrong. Grief is in store for us, but let us not be enemies."

Mournfully, he gave his hand to Arthur, and Oriana, as she wakened from her trance, beheld them locked in that sad grasp, like two twin statues of despair.

They led her to the house, and then the two young men walked out alone, and talked frankly and tranquilly upon the subject. It was determined that both should leave Riverside manor on the morrow, and that Oriana should be left to commune with her own heart, and take counsel of time and meditation. They would not grieve Beverly with their secret, at least not for the present, when his sister was so ill prepared to bear remonstrance or reproof. Harold wrote a kind letter for Oriana, in which he released her from her pledged faith, asking only that she should take time to study her heart, but in no wise let a sense of duty stand in the way of her happiness. He took pains to conceal the depth of his own affliction, and to avoid whatever she might construe as reproach.

They would have gone without an interview with Oriana, but that would have seemed strange to Beverly. However, Oriana, although pale and nervous, met them in the morning with more composure than they had anticipated. Harold, just before starting, drew her aside, and placed the letter in her hand.

"That will tell you all I would say, and you must read it when your heart is strong and firm. Do not look so wretched. All may yet be well. I would fain see you smile before I go."

But though she had evidently nerved herself to be composed, the tears would come, and her heart seemed rising to her throat and about to burst in sobs.

"I will be your true wife, Harold, and I will love you. Do not desert me, do not cast me from you. I cannot bear to be so guilty. Indeed, Harold, I will be true and faithful to you."

There is no guilt in that young heart," he answered, as he kissed her forehead. "But now, we must not talk of love; hereafter, perhaps, when time and absence shall teach us where to choose for happiness. Part from me now as if I were your brother, and give me a sister's kiss. Would you see Arthur?"

She trembled and whispered painfully:

"No, Harold, no—I dare not. Oh, Harold, bid him forget me."

"It is better that you should not see him. Farewell! be brave. We are good friends, remember. Farewell, dear girl."

Beverly had been waiting with the carriage, and as the time was short, he called to Harold. Arthur, who stood at the carriage wheel, simply raised his hat to Oriana, as if in a parting salute. He would have given his right hand to have pressed hers for a moment; but his will was iron, and he did not once look back as the carriage whirled away.

CHAPTER X

In the drawing-room of an elegant mansion in a fashionable quarter of the city of New York, toward the close of April, a social party were assembled, distributed mostly in small conversational groups. The head of the establishment, a pompous, well-to-do merchant, stout, short, and baldheaded, and evidently well satisfied with himself and his position in society, was vehemently expressing his opinions upon the affairs of the nation to an attentive audience of two or three elderly business men, with a ponderous earnestness that proved him, in his own estimation, as much *au fait* in political affairs as in the routine of his counting-room. An individual of middle age, a man of the world, apparently, who was seated at a side-table, carelessly glancing over a book of engravings, was the only one who occasionally exasperated the pompous gentleman with contradictions or ill-timed interruptions.

"The government must be sustained," said the stout gentleman, "and we, the merchants of the North, will do it. It is money, sir, money," he continued, unconsciously rattling the coin in his breeches pocket, "that settles every question at the present day, and our money will bring these beggarly rebels to their senses. They can't do without us, sir. They would be ruined in six months, if shut out from commercial intercourse with the North."

"How long before you would be ruined by the operations of the same cause?" inquired the individual at the side-table.

"Sir, we of the North hold the wealth of the country in our pockets. They can't fight against our money—they can't do it, sir."

"Your ancestors fought against money, and fought passably well."

"Yes, sir, for the great principles of human liberty."

"Which these rebels believe they are fighting for. You have need of all your money to keep a respectable army in the field. These Southerners may have to fight in rags, as insurgents generally do: witness the struggle of your Revolution; but until you lay waste their corn-fields and drive off their cattle, they will have full stomachs, and that, after all, is the first consideration."

"You are an alien, sir, a foreigner; you know nothing of our great institutions; you know nothing of the wealth of the North, and the spirit of the people."

"I see a great deal of bunting in the streets, and hear any quantity of declamation at your popular gatherings. But as I journeyed northward from New Orleans, I saw the same in the South—perhaps more of it."

"And could not distinguish between the frenzy of treason and the enthusiasm of patriotism?"

"Not at all; except that treason seemed more earnest and unanimous."

"You have seen with the eyes of an Englishman—of one hostile to our institutions."

"Oh, no; as a man of the world, a traveller, without prejudice or passion, receiving impressions and noting them. I like your country; I like your people. I have observed foibles in the North and in the South, but there is an under-current of strong feeling and good sense which I have noted and admired. I think your quarrel is one of foibles—one conceived in the spirit of petulance, and about to be prosecuted in the spirit of exaltation. I believe the professed mutual hatred of the sections to be superficial, and that it could be cancelled. It is fostered by the bitterness of fanatics, assisted by a very natural disinclination on the part of the masses to yield a disputed point. If hostilities should cease to-morrow, you would be better friends than ever."

"But the principle, sir! The right of the thing, and the wrong of the thing! Can we parley with traitors? Can we negotiate with armed rebellion? Is it not our paramount duty to set at rest forever the doctrine of secession?"

"As a matter of policy, perhaps. But as a right, I doubt it. Your government I look upon as a mere agency appointed by contracting parties to transact certain affairs for their convenience. Should one or more of those contracting parties, sovereignties in themselves, hold it to their interest to transact their business without the assistance of an agent, I cannot perceive that the right can be denied by any provision of the contract. In your case, the employers have dismissed their agent, who seeks to reinstate the office by force of arms. As justly might my lawyer, when I no longer need his services, attempt to coerce me into a continuance of business relations, by invading my residence with a loaded pistol. The States, without extinguishing their sovereignty, created the Federal Government; it is the child of State legislation, and now the child seeks to chastise and control the parent. The General Government can possess no inherent or self-created function; its power, its very existence, were granted for certain uses. As regards your State's connection with that Government, no other State has the right to interfere; but as for another State's connection with it, the power that made it can unmake."

"So you would have the government quietly acquiesce in the robbery of public property, the occupation of Federal strongholds and the seizure of ships and revenues in which they have but a share?"

"If, by the necessity of the case, the seceded States hold in their possession more than their share of public property, a division should be made by arbitration, as in other cases where a distribution of common property is required. It may have been a wrong and an insult to bombard Fort Sumter and haul down the Federal flag, but that does not establish a right on the part of the Federal Government to coerce the wrong-doing States into a union with the others. And that, I take it, is the avowed purpose of your administration."

"Yes, and that purpose will be fulfilled. We have the money to do it, and we will do it, sir."

A tall, thin gentleman, with a white cravat and a bilious complexion, approached the party from a different part of the room.

"It can't be done with money, Mr. Pursely," said the new comer, "Unless the great, the divine principle of universal human liberty is invoked. An offended but merciful Providence has given the people this chance for redemption, in the opportunity to strike the shackle from the slave. I hold the war a blessing to the nation and to humanity, in that it will cleanse the land from its curse of slavery. It is an invitation from God to wipe away the record of our past tardiness and tolerance, by striking at the great sin with fire and sword. The blood of millions is nothing—the woe, the lamentation, the ruin of the land is nothing—the overthrow of the Union itself is nothing, if we can but win God's smile by setting a brand in the hand of the bondman to scourge his master. But assuredly unless we arouse the slave to seize the torch and the dagger, and avenge the wrongs of his race, Providence will frown upon our efforts, and our arms will not prevail."

A tall man in military undress replied with considerable emphasis:

"Then your black-coated gentry must fight their own battle. The people will not arm if abolition is to be the watchword. I for one will not strike a blow if it be not understood that the institutions of the South shall be respected."

"The government must be sustained, that is the point," cried Mr. Pursely. "It matters little what becomes of the negro, but the government must be sustained. Otherwise, what security will there be for property, and what will become of trade?"

"Who thinks of trade or property at such a crisis?" interrupted an enthusiast, in figured trowsers and a gay cravat. "Our beloved Union must and shall be preserved. The fabric that our fathers reared for us must not be allowed to crumble. We will prop it with our mangled bodies," and he brushed a speck of dust from the fine broadcloth of his sleeve.

"The insult to our flag must be wiped out," said the military gentleman. "The honor of the glorious stripes and stars must be vindicated to the world."

"Let us chastise these boasting Southrons," said another, "and prove our supremacy in arms, and I shall be satisfied."

"But above all," insisted a third, "we must check the sneers and exultation of European powers, and show them that we have not forgotten the art of war since the days of 1776 and 1812."

"I should like to know what you are going to fight about," said the Englishman, quietly; "for there appears to be much diversity of opinion. However, if you are determined to cut each others' throats, perhaps one pretext is as good as another, and a dozen better than only one."

In the quiet recess of a window, shadowed by the crimson curtains, sat a fair young girl, and a man, young and handsome, but upon whose countenance the traces of dissipation and of passion were deeply marked. Miranda Ayleff was a Virginian, the cousin and quondam playmate of Oriana Weems, like her an orphan, and a ward of Beverly. Her companion was Philip Searle. She had known him in Richmond, and had become much attached to him, but his habits and character were such, that her friends, and Beverly chiefly, had earnestly discouraged their intimacy. Philip left for the North, and Miranda, who at the date of our story was the guest of Mrs. Pursely, her relative, met him in New York, after a separation of two years. Philip, who, in spite of his evil ways, was singularly handsome and agreeable in manners, found little difficulty in fanning the old flame, and, upon the plea of old acquaintance, became a frequent visitor upon Miranda at Mr. Pursely's mansion, where we now find them, earnestly conversing, but in low tones, in the little solitude of the great bay window.

"You reproach me with vices which your unkindness has helped to stain me with. Driven from your presence, whom alone I cared to live for, what marvel if I sought oblivion in the wine-cup and the dice-box? Give me one chance, Miranda, to redeem myself. Let me call you wife, and you will become my guardian angel, and save me from myself."

"You know that I love you, Philip," she replied, "and willingly would I share your destiny, hoping to win you from evil. Go with me to Richmond. We will speak with Beverly, who is kind and truly loves me. We will convince him of your good purposes, and will win his consent to our union."

"No, Miranda; Beverly and your friends in Richmond will never believe me worthy of you. Besides, it would be dangerous for me to visit Richmond. I have identified myself with the Northern cause, and although, for your sake, I might refrain from bearing arms against Virginia, yet I have little sympathy with any there, where I have been branded as a drunkard and a gambler."

"Yet, Philip, is it not the land of your birth—the home of your boyhood?"

"The land of my shame and humiliation. No, Miranda, I will not return to Virginia. And if you love me, you will not return. What are these senseless quarrels to us? We can be happy in each other's love, and forget that madmen are at war around us. Why will you not trust me, Miranda—why do you thus withhold from me my only hope of redemption from the terrible vice that is killing me? I put my destiny, my very life in your keeping, and you hesitate to accept the trust that alone can save me. Oh, Miranda! you do not love me."

"Philip, I cannot renounce my friends, my dear country, the home of my childhood."

"Then look you what will be my fate: I will join the armies of the North, and fling away my life in battle against my native soil. Ruin and death cannot come too soon when you forsake me."

Miranda remained silent, but, through the gloom of the recess, he could see the glistening of a tear upon her cheek.

The hall-bell rang, and the servant brought in a card for Miss Ayleff. Following it, Arthur Wayne was ushered into the room.

She rose to receive him, somewhat surprised at a visit from a stranger.

"I have brought these letters for you from my good friend Beverly Weems," said Arthur. "At his request, I have ventured to call in person, most happy, if you will forgive the presumption, in the opportunity."

She gave her hand, and welcomed him gracefully and warmly, and, having introduced Mr. Searle, excused herself while she glanced at the contents of Beverly's letter. While thus employed, Arthur marked her changing color; and then, lifting his eyes lest his scrutiny might be rude, observed Philip's dark eye fixed upon her with a suspicious and searching expression. Then Philip looked up, and their glances met—the calm blue eye and the flashing black—but for an instant, but long enough to confirm the instinctive feeling that there was no sympathy between their hearts.

A half-hour's general conversation ensued, but Philip appeared restless and uneasy, and rose to take his leave. She followed him to the parlor door.

"Come to me to-morrow," she said, as she gave her hand, "and we will talk again."

A smile of triumph rested upon his pale lips for a second; but he pressed her hand, and, murmuring an affectionate farewell, withdrew.

Arthur remained a few moments, but observing that Miranda was pensive and absent, he bade her good evening, accepting her urgent invitation to call at an early period.

CHAPTER XI.

"Well, Arthur," said Harold Hare, entering the room of the former at his hotel, on the following evening, "I have come to bid you good bye. I start for home to-morrow morning," he added, in reply to Arthur's questioning glance. "I am to have a company of Providence boys in my old friend Colonel R——'s regiment. And after a little brisk recruiting, ho! for Washington and the wars!"

"You have determined for the war, then?"

"Of course. And you?"

"I shall go to my Vermont farm, and live quietly among my books and pastures."

"A dull life, Arthur, when every wind that blows will bring to your ears the swell of martial music and the din of arms."

"If I were in love with the pomp of war, which, thank heaven, I am not, Harold, I would rather dwell in a hermit's cave, than follow the fife and drum over the bodies of my Southern countrymen."

"Those Southern countrymen, that you seem to love better than the country they would ruin, would have little remorse in marching over your body, even among the ashes of your farm-house. Doubtless you would stand at your threshold, and welcome their butchery, should their ruffian legions ravage our land as far as your Green Mountains."

"I do not think they will invade one foot of Northern soil, unless compelled by strict military necessity. However, should the State to which I owe allegiance be attacked by foreign or domestic foe, I will stand among its defenders. But, dear Harold, let us not argue this sad subject, which it is grief enough but to contemplate. Tell me of your plans, and how I shall communicate with you, while you are absent. My distress about this unhappy war will be keener, when I feel that my dear friend may be its victim."

Harold pressed his hand affectionately, and the two friends spoke of the misty future, till Harold arose to depart. They had not mentioned Oriana's name, though she was in their thoughts, and each, as he bade farewell, knew that some part of the other's sadness was for her sake.

Arthur accompanied Harold a short distance up Broadway, and returning, found at the office of the hotel, a letter, without post-mark, to his address. He stepped into the reading-room to peruse it. It was from Beverly, and ran thus:

"RICHMOND, *May* —, 1861.

"DEAR ARTHUR: The departure of a friend gives me an opportunity to write you about a matter that I beg you will attend to, for my sake, thoroughly. I learned this morning, upon receipt of a letter from Mr. Pursely, that Miranda Ayleff, of whom we spoke together, and to whom I presume you have already delivered my communication, is receiving the visits of one Philip Searle, to whom, some two years since, she was much attached. *Entre nous*, Arthur, I can tell you, the man is a scoundrel of the deepest dye. Not only a drunkard and a gambler, but dishonest, and unfit for any decent girl's society. He is guilty of forgery against me, and, against my conscience, I hushed the matter only out of consideration for her feelings. I would still have concealed the matter from her, had this resumption of their intimacy not occurred. But her welfare must cancel all scruples of that character; and I therefore entreat you to see her at once, and unmask the man fully and unequivocally. If necessary you may show my letter for that purpose. I would go on to New York myself immediately, were I not employed upon a State mission of exceeding delicacy and importance; but I have full confidence in your good judgment. Spare no arguments to induce her to return immediately to Richmond.

"Oriana has not been well; I know not what ails her, but, though she makes no complaint, the girl seems really ill. She knows not of my writing, for I would not pain her about Miranda, of whom she is very fond. But I can venture, without consulting her, to send you her good wishes. Let me hear from you in full about what I have written.   Your friend.
"BEVERLY WEEMS."

"P. S.—Knowing that you must yet be weak with your late illness, I would have troubled Harold, rather than you, about this matter, but I am ignorant of his present whereabouts, while I know that you contemplated remaining a week or so in New York. Write me about the ugly bite in the shoulder, from which I trust you are well recovered.   B. W."

Arthur looked up from the letter, and beheld Philip Searle seated at the opposite side of the table. He had entered while Arthur's attention was absorbed in reading, and having glanced at the address of the envelope which lay upon the table, he recognized the hand of Beverly. This prompted him to pause, and taking up one of the newspapers which were strewn about the table, he sat down, and while he appeared to read, glanced furtively at his *vis-à-vis* over the paper's edge. When his presence was noticed, he bowed, and Arthur, with a slight and stern inclination of the head, fixed his calm eye upon him with a searching severity that brought a flush of anger to Philip's brow.

"That is Weems' hand," he muttered, inwardly, "and by that fellow's look, I fancy that no less a person than myself is the subject of his epistle."

Arthur had walked away, but, in his surprise at the unexpected presence of Searle, he had allowed the letter to remain upon the table. No sooner had he passed out of the room, than Philip quietly but rapidly stretched his hand beneath the pile of scattered journals, and drew it toward him. It required but an instant for his quick eye to catch the substance. His face grew livid, and his teeth grated harshly with suppressed rage.

"We shall have a game of plot and counter-plot before this ends, my man," he muttered.

There were pen and paper on the table, and he wrote a few lines hastily, placed them in the envelope, and put Beverly's letter in his pocket. He had hardly finished when Arthur reëntered the room, advanced rapidly to the table, and, with a look of relief, took up the envelope and its contents, and again left the room. Philip's lip curled beneath the black moustache with a smile of triumphant malice.

"Keep it safe in your pocket for a few hours, my gamecock, and my heiress to a beggar-girl, I'll have stone walls between you and me."

CHAPTER XII.

The evening was somewhat advanced, but Arthur determined at once to seek an interview with Miss Ayleff. Hastily arranging his toilet, he walked briskly up Broadway, revolving in his mind a fit course for fulfilling his delicate errand.

To shorten his way, he turned into a cross street in the upper part of the city. As he approached the hall door of a large brick house, his eye chanced to fall upon a man who was ringing for admittance. The light from the street lamp fell full upon his face, and he recognized the features of Philip Searle. At that moment the door was opened, and Philip entered. Arthur would have passed on, but something in the appearance of the house arrested his attention, and, on closer scrutiny, revealed to him its character. One of those impulses which sometimes sway our actions, tempted him to enter, and learn, if possible, something further respecting the habits of the man whose scheme he had been commissioned to thwart. A moment's reflection might have changed his purpose, but his hand was already upon the bell, and the summons was quickly answered by a good-looking but faded young woman, with painted cheeks and gay attire. She fixed her keen, bold eyes upon him for a few seconds, and then, tossing her ringlets, pertly invited him to enter.

"Who is within?" asked Arthur, standing in the hall.

"Only the girls. Walk in."

"The gentleman who came in before me, is he there?"

"Do you want to see him?" she asked, suspiciously.

"Oh, no. Only I would avoid being seen by any one."

"He will not see you. Come right in." And she threw open the door, and flaunted in.

Arthur followed her without hesitation.

Bursts of forced and cheerless laughter, and the shrill sound of rude and flippant talk, smote unpleasantly upon his ear. The room was richly furnished, but without taste or modesty. The tall mirrors were displayed with ostentation, and the paintings, offensive in design, hung conspicuous in showy frames. The numerous gas jets, flashing among glittering crystal pendants, made vice more glaring and heartlessness more terribly apparent. Women, with bold and haggard eyes, with brazen brows, and cheeks from which the roses of virgin shame had been plucked to bloom no more forever—mostly young girls, scourging their youth into old age, and gathering poison at once for soul and body —with sensual indolence reclined upon the rich ottomans, or with fantastic grace whirled through lewd waltzes over the velvet carpets. There was laughter without joy—there was frivolity without merriment—there was the surface of enjoyment and the substance of woe, for beneath those painted cheeks was the pallor of despair and broken health, and beneath those whitened bosoms, half veiled with gaudy silks, were hearts that were aching with remorse, or, yet more unhappy, benumbed and callous with habitual sin.

Yet there, like a crushed pearl upon a heap of

garbage, lingers the trace of beauty; and there, surely, though sepulchred in the caverns of vice, dwells something that was once innocence, and not unredeemable. But whence is the friendly word to come, whence the guardian hand that might lift them from the slough. They live accursed by even charity, shunned by philanthropy, and shut from the Christian world like a tribe of lepers whose touch is contagion and whose breath is pestilence. In the glittering halls of fashion, the high-born beauty, with wreaths about her white temples and diamonds upon her chaste bosom, gives her gloved hand for the dance, and forgets that an erring sister, by the touch of those white fingers, might be raised from the grave of her chastity, and clothed anew with the white garments of repentance. But no; the cold world of fashion, that from its cushioned pew has listened with stately devotion to the words of the Redeemer, has taught her that to redeem the fallen is beneath her caste. The bond of sisterhood is broken. The lost one must pursue her hideous destiny, each avenue of escape blocked by the scorn and loathing which denies her the contact of virtue and the counsel of purity. In the broad fields of charity, invaded by cold philosophers, losing themselves in searching unreal and vague philanthropies, none so practical in beneficence as to take her by the hand, saying, "Go, and sin no more."

But whenever the path of benevolence is intricate and doubtful, whenever the work is linked with a riddle whose solving will breed discord and trouble among men, whenever there is a chance to make philanthropy a plea for hate, and bitterness and charity can be made a battle-cry to arouse the spirit of destruction, and spread ruin and desolation over the fair face of the earth, then will the domes of our churches resound with eloquence, then will the journals of the land teem with their mystic theories, then will the mourners of human woe be loud in lamentation, and lift up their mighty voices to cry down an abstract evil. When actual misery appeals to them, they are deaf; when the plain and palpable error stalks before them, they turn aside. They are too busy with the tangles of some philanthropic Gordian knot, to stretch out a helping hand to the sufferer at their sides. They are frenzied with their zeal to build a bridge over a spanless ocean, while the drowning wretch is sinking within their grasp. They scorn the simple charity of the good Samaritan; theirs must be a gigantic and splendid achievement in experimental beneficence, worthy of their philosophic brains. The wrong they would redress must be one that half the world esteems a right; else there would be no room for their arguments, no occasion for their invective, no excuse for their passion. To do good is too simple for their transcendentalism; they must first make evil out of their logic, and then, through blood and wasting flames, drive on the people to destruction, that the imaginary evil may be destroyed. While Charity soars so high among the clouds, she will never stoop to lift the Magdalen from sin.

CHAPTER XIII.

Arthur heaved an involuntary sigh, as he gazed upon those sad wrecks of womanhood, striving to harden their sense of degradation by its impudent display. But an expression of bewildered and sorrowful surprise suddenly overspread his countenance. Seated alone upon a cushioned stool, at the chimney-corner, was a young woman, her elbows resting upon her knees, and her face bent thoughtfully upon her palms. She was apparently lost in thought to all around her. She was thinking—of what? Perhaps of the green fields where she played in childhood; perhaps of her days of innocence; perhaps of the mother at whose feet she had once knelt in prayer. But she was far away, in thought, from that scene of infamy of which she was a part; for, in the glare of the gaslight, a tear struggled through her eyelashes, and glittered like a ray from heaven piercing the glooms of hell.

Arthur walked to her, and placed his hand softly upon her yellow hair.

"Oh, Mary!" he murmured, in a tone of gentle sorrow, that sounded strangely amid the discordant merriment that filled the room.

She looked up, at his touch, but when his voice fell upon her ear, she arose suddenly and stood before him like one struck dumb betwixt humiliation and wonder. The angel had not yet fled that bosom, for the blush of shame glowed through the chalk upon her brow and outcrimsoned the paint upon her cheek. As it passed away, she would have wreathed her lip mechanically with the pert smile of her vocation, but the smile was frozen ere it reached her lips, and the coarse words she would have spoken died into a murmur and a sob. She sank down again upon the cushion, and bent her face low down upon her hands.

"Oh, Mary! is it you! is it you! I pray heaven your mother be in her grave!"

She rose and escaped quickly from the room; but he followed her and checked her at the stairway.

"Let me speak with you, Mary. No, not here; lead me to your room."

He followed her up-stairs, and closing the door, sat beside her as she leaned upon the bed and buried her face in the pillow.

It was the child of his old nurse. Upon the hill-sides of his native State they had played together when children, and now she lay there before him, with scarce enough of woman's nature left to weep for her own misery.

"Mary, how is this? Look up, child," he said, taking her hand kindly. "I had rather see you thus, bent low with sorrow, than bold and hard in guilt. But yet look up and speak to me. I will be your friend, you know. Tell me, why are you thus?"

"Oh, Mr. Wayne, do not scold me, please don't. I was thinking of home and mother when you came and put your hand on my head. Mother's dead."

"Well for her, poor woman. But how came you thus?'

"I scarcely seem to know. It seems to me a dream. I married John, and he brought me to New York. Then the war came, and he went and was killed. And mother was dead, and I had no friends in the great city. I could get no work, and I was starving, indeed I was, Mr.

Wayne. So a young man, who was very handsome, and rich, I think, for he gave me money and fine dresses, he promised me —— Oh, Mr. Wayne, I was very wrong and foolish, and I wish I could die, and be buried by my poor mother."

" And did he bring you here?"

" Oh no, sir. I came here two weeks ago, after he had left me. And when he came in one night and found me here, he was very angry, and said he would kill me if I told any one that I knew him. And I know why; but you won't tell, Mr. Wayne, for it would make him angry. I have found out that he is married to the mistress of this house. He's a bad man, I know now, and often comes here drunk, and swears at the woman and the girls. Hark! that's her room, next to mine, and I think he's in there now."

The faint sound of voices, smothered by the walls, reached them from the adjoining chamber; but as they listened, the door of that room opened, and the loud and angry tones of a man, speaking at the threshold, could be distinctly heard. Arthur quietly and carefully opened the door of Mary's room, an inch or less, and listened at the aperture. He was not mistaken; he recognized the voice of Philip Searle.

"I'll do it, anyhow," said Philip, angrily, and with the thick utterance of one who had been drinking. "I'll do it; and if you trouble me, I'll fix you."

"Philip, if you marry that girl I'll peach; I will, so help me G—d," replied a woman's voice. "I've given you the money, and I've given you plenty before, as much as I had to give you, Philip, and you know it. I don't mind that, but you shan't marry till I'm dead. I'm your lawful wife, and if I'm low now, it's your fault, for you drove me to it."

"I'll drive you to hell if you worry me. I tell you she's got lots of money, and a farm, and niggers, and you shall have half if you only keep your mouth shut. Come, now, Molly, don't be a fool; what's the use, now?"

They went down the stairway together, and their voices were lost as they descended. Arthur determined to follow and get some clue, if possible, as to the man's intentions. He therefore gave his address to Mary, and made her promise faithfully to meet him on the following morning, promising to befriend her and send her to his mother in Vermont. Hearing the front door close, and surmising that Philip had departed, he bade her good night, and descending hastily, was upon the sidewalk in time to observe Philip's form in the starlight as he turned the corner.

It was now ten o'clock; too late to call upon Miranda without disturbing the household, which he desired to avoid. Arthur's present fear was that possibly an elopement had been planned for that night, and he therefore determined, if practicable, to keep Searle in view till he had traced him home. The latter entered a refreshment saloon upon Broadway; Arthur followed, and ordering, in a low tone, some dish that would require time in the preparation, he stepped, without noise, into an alcove adjoining one whence came the sound of conversation.

"Well, what's up?" inquired a gruff, coarse voice.

"Fill me some brandy," replied Philip. "I tell you, Bradshaw, it's risky, but I'll do it.

The old woman's rock. She'll blow upon me if she gets the chance; but I'm in for it, and I'll put it through. We must manage to keep it mum from her, and as soon as I get the girl I'll accept the lieutenancy, and be off to the wars till all blows over. If Moll should smoke me out there, I'll cross the line and take sanctuary with Jeff. Davis.

"What about the girl?"

"Oh, she's all right," replied Philip, with a drunken chuckle. "I had an interview with the dear creature this morning, and she's like wax in my hands. It's all arranged for to-morrow morning. You be sure to have the carriage ready at the Park—the same spot, you know—by ten o'clock. She can't well get away before, but that will be time enough for the train."

"I want that money now."

"Moll's hard up, but I got a couple of hundred from her. Here's fifty for you; now don't grumble, I'm doing the best I can, d—n you, and you know it. Now listen—I want to fix things with you about that blue-eyed chap."

The waiter here brought in Arthur's order,

and a sudden silence ensued in the alcove. The two men had evidently been unaware of the proximity of a third party, and their tone, though low, had not been sufficiently guarded to escape Arthur hearing, whose ear, leaning against the thin partition, was within a few inches of Philip's head. A muttered curse and the gurgling of liquor from a decanter was all that could be heard for the space of a few moments, when the two, after a brief whisper, arose and left the place, not, however, without making ineffectual efforts to catch a glimpse of the occupant of the tenanted alcove. Arthur soon after followed them into the street. He was aware that he was watched from the opposite corner, and that his steps were dogged in the darkness. But he drew his felt hat well over his face, and by mingling with the crowd that chanced to be pouring from one of the theatres, he avoided recognition and passed unnoticed into his hotel.

CHAPTER XIV.

ARTHUR felt ill and much fatigued when he retired to rest, and was restless and disturbed with fever throughout the night. He had overtasked his delicate frame, yet scarce recovered from the effects of recent suffering, and he arose in the morning with a feeling of prostration that he could with difficulty overcome. However, he refreshed himself with a cup of tea, and prepared to call upon Miss Ayleff. It was but seven o'clock, a somewhat early hour for a morning visit, but the occasion was one for little ceremony. As he was on the point of leaving his room, there was a peremptory knock at the door, and, upon his invitation to walk in, a stranger entered. It was a gentlemanly personage, with a searching eye and a calm and quiet manner. Arthur was vexed to be delayed, but received the intruder with a civil inclination of the head, somewhat surprised, however, that no card had been sent to give him intimation of the visit.

"Are you Mr. Arthur Wayne?" inquired the stranger.

"I am he," replied Arthur. "Be seated, sir."

"I thank you. My name is ———. I am a deputy United States marshal of this district."

Arthur bowed, and awaited a further statement of the purpose of his visit.

"You have lately arrived from Virginia, I understand?"

"A few days since, sir—from a brief sojourn in the vicinity of Richmond."

"And yesterday received a communication from that quarter?"

"I did. A letter from an intimate acquaintance."

"My office will excuse me from an imputation of inquisitiveness. May I see that letter?"

"Excuse me, sir. Its contents are of a private and delicate nature, and intended only for my own perusal."

"It is because its contents are of that nature that I am constrained to ask you for it. Pardon me, Mr. Wayne; but to be brief and frank with you, I must either receive that communication by your good will, or call in my officers, and institute a search. I am sure you will not make my duty more unpleasant than necessary."

Arthur paused awhile. He was conscious that it would be impossible for him to avoid complying with the marshal's request, and yet it was most annoying to be obliged to make a third party cognizant of the facts contained in Beverly's epistle.

"I have no desire to oppose you in the performance of your functions," he finally replied, "but really there are very particular reasons why the contents of this letter should not be made public."

A very faint indication of a smile passed over the marshal's serious face; Arthur did not observe it, but continued:

"I will hand you the letter, for I perceive there has been some mistake and misapprehension which of course it is your duty to clear up. But you must promise me that, when your perusal of it shall have satisfied you that its nature is strictly private, and not offensive to the law, you will return it me and preserve an inviolable secrecy as to its contents."

"When I shall be satisfied on that score, I will do as you desire."

Arthur handed him the letter, somewhat to the other's surprise, for he had certainly been watching for an attempt at its destruction, or at least was prepared for prevarication and stratagem. He took the paper from its envelope and read it carefully. It was in the following words:

RICHMOND, May —, 1861.

DEAR ARTHUR: This will be handed to you by a sure hand. Communicate freely with the bearer—he can be trusted. The arms can be safely shipped as he represents, and you will therefore send them on at once. Your last communication was of great service to the cause, and, although I would be glad to have you with us, the President thinks you are too valuable, for the present, where you are. When you come, the commission will be ready for you.   Yours truly,

BEVERLY WEEMS, Capt. C. S. A.

"Are you satisfied?" inquired Arthur, after the marshal had silently concluded his examination of the document.

"Perfectly satisfied," replied the other, placing the letter in his pocket. "Mr. Wayne, it is my duty to arrest you."

"Arrest me!"

"In the name of the United States."

"For what offence?"

"Treason."

Arthur remained for a while silent with astonishment. At last, as the marshal arose and took his hat, he said:

"I cannot conceive what act or word of mine can be construed as treasonable. There is some mistake, surely; I am a quiet man, a stranger in the city, and have conversed with but one or two persons since my arrival. Explain to me, if you please, the particular nature of the charge against me.

"It is not my province, at this moment, to do so, Mr. Wayne. It is sufficient that, upon information lodged with me last evening, and forwarded to Washington by telegraph, I received from the Secretary of War orders for your immediate arrest, should I find the information true. I have found it true, and I arrest you."

"Surely, nothing in that letter can be so misconstrued as to implicate me."

"Mr. Wayne, this prevarication is as useless as it is unseemly. You *know* that the letter is sufficient warrant for my proceeding. My carriage is at the door. I trust you will accompany me without further delay."

"Sir, I was about to proceed, when you entered, upon an errand that involves the safety and happiness of the young lady mentioned in that letter. The letter itself will inform you of the circumstance, and I assure you, events are in progress that require my immediate action. You will at least allow me to visit the party?"

The marshal looked at him with surprise.

"What party?"

"The lady of whom my friend makes mention."

"I do not understand you. I can only conceive that, for some purpose of your own, you are anxious to gain time. I must request you to accompany me at once to the carriage."

"You will permit me at least to send a letter—a word—a warning?"

"That your accomplice may receive information? Assuredly not."

" Be yourself the messenger—or send "——

"This subterfuge is idle." He opened the door and stood beside it. "I must request your company to the carriage."

Arthur's cheek flushed for a moment with anger.

"This severity," he said, "is ridiculous and unjust. I tell you, you and those for whom you act will be accountable for a great crime—for innocence betrayed—for a young life made desolate—for perhaps a dishonored grave. I plead not for myself, but for one helpless and pure, who at this hour may be the victim of a villain's plot. In the name of humanity, I entreat you give me but time to avert the calamity, and I will follow you without remonstrance. Go with me yourself. Be present at the interview. Of what consequence to you will be an hour's delay?"

"It may be of much consequence to those who are in league with you. I cannot grant your request. You must come with me, sir, or I shall be obliged to call for assistance," and he drew a pair of handcuffs from his pocket.

Arthur perceived that further argument or entreaty would be of no avail. He was much agitated and distressed beyond measure at the possible misfortune to Miranda, which, by this untimely arrest, he was powerless to avert. Knowing nothing of the true contents of the letter which Philip had substituted for the one received from Beverly, he could not imagine an excuse for the marshal's inflexibility. He was quite ill, too, and what with fever and agitation, his brain was in a whirl. He leaned against the chair, faint and dispirited. The painful cough, the harbinger of that fatal malady which had already brought a sister to an early grave, oppressed him, and the hectic glowed upon his pale cheeks. The marshal approached him, and laid his hand gently on his shoulder.

"You seem ill," he said; "I am sorry to be harsh with you, but I must do my duty. They will make you as comfortable as possible at the fort. But you must come."

Arthur followed him mechanically, and like one in a dream. They stepped into the carriage and were driven rapidly away; but Arthur, as he leaned back exhausted in his seat, murmured sorrowfully:

"And poor little Mary, too! Who will befriend her now?"

CHAPTER XV.

In the upper apartment of a cottage standing alone by the roadside on the outskirts of Boston, Miranda, pale and dejected, sat gazing vacantly at the light of the solitary lamp that lit the room. The clock was striking midnight, and the driving rain beat dismally against the window-blinds. But one month had passed since her elopement with Philip Searle, yet her wan cheeks and altered aspect revealed how much of suffering can be crowded into that little space of time. She started from her revery when the striking of the timepiece told the lateness of the hour. Heavy footsteps sounded upon the stairway, and, while she listened, Philip, followed by Bradshaw, entered the room abruptly.

"How is this?" asked Philip, angrily. "Why are you not in bed?"

"I did not know it was so late, Philip," she answered, in a deprecating tone. "I was half asleep upon the rocking-chair, listening to the storm. It's a bad night, Philip. How wet you are!"

He brushed off the hand she had laid upon his shoulder, and muttered, with bad humor:

"I've told you a dozen times I don't want you to sit up for me. Fetch the brandy and glasses, and go to bed."

"Oh, Philip, it is so late! Don't drink to-night, Philip. You are wet, and you look tired. Come to bed."

"Do as I tell you," he answered, roughly, flinging himself into a chair, and beckoning Bradshaw to a seat. Miranda sighed, and brought the bottle and glasses from the closet.

"Now, you go to sleep, do you hear; and don't be whining and crying all night, like a sick girl."

The poor girl moved slowly to the door, and turned at the threshold.

"Good night, Philip."

"Oh, good night—there, get along," he cried, impatiently, without looking at her, and gulping down a tumblerful of spirits. Miranda closed the door, and left the two men alone together.

They remained silent for a while, Bradshaw quietly sipping his liquor, and Philip evidently disturbed and angry.

"You're sure 'twas she?" he asked at last.

"Oh, bother!" replied Bradshaw. "I'm not a mole nor a blind man. Don't I know Moll when I see her?"

"Curse her! she'll stick to me like a leech. What could have brought her here? Do you think she's tracked me?"

"She'd track you through fire, if she once got on the scent. Moll ain't the gal to be fooled, and you know it."

"What's to be done?"

"Move out of this. Take the girl to Virginia. You'll be safe enough there."

"You're right, Bradshaw. It's the best way. I ought to have done it at first. But, hang the girl, she'll weary me to death with her sermons and crying fits. Moll's worth two of her for that matter—she scolds, but at least she never would look like a stuck fawn when I came home a little queer. For the matter of that, she don't mind a spree herself at times." And, emptying his glass, the libertine laughed at the remembrance of some past orgies.

While he was thus, in his half-drunken mood, consoling himself for present perplexities by dwelling upon the bacchanalian joys of other days, a carriage drove up the street, and stopped before the door. Soon afterward, the hall bell was rung, and Philip, alarmed and astonished, started from his seat.

"Who's that?" he asked, almost in a whisper.

"Don't know," replied his companion.

"She couldn't have traced me here already—unless you have betrayed me, Bradshaw," he added suddenly, darting a suspicious glance upon his comrade.

"You're just drunk enough to be a fool," replied Bradshaw, rising from his seat, as a second summons, more violent than the first, echoed through the corridors. "I'll go down and see what's the matter. Some one's mistaken the house, I suppose. That's all."

"Let no one in, Bradshaw," cried Philip, as that worthy left the room. He descended the stairs, opened the door, and presently afterward the carriage drove rapidly away. Philip, who had been listening earnestly, could hear the sound of the wheels as they whirled over the pavement.

"All right," he said, as he applied himself once more to the bottle before him. "Some fool has mistaken his whereabouts. Curse me, but I'm getting as nervous as an old woman."

He was in the act of lifting the glass to his lips, when the door was flung wide open. The glass fell from his hands, and shivered upon the floor. Moll stood before him.

She stood at the threshold with a wicked gleam in her eye, and a smile of triumph upon her lips; then advanced into the room, closed the door quietly, locked it, seated herself composedly in the nearest chair, and filled herself a glass of spirits. Philip glared upon her with an expression of mingled anger, fear and wonderment.

"Are you a devil? Where in thunder did you spring from?" he asked at last.

"You'll make me a devil, with your tricks, Philip Searle," she said, sipping the liquor, and looking at him wickedly over the rim of the tumbler.

"Ha! ha! ha!" she laughed aloud, as he

muttered a curse between his clenched teeth, "I'm not the country girl, Philip dear, that I was when you whispered your sweet nonsense in my ear. I know your game, my bully boy, and I'll play you card for card."

"Bradshaw!" shouted Philip, going to the door and striving to open it.

"It's no use," she said. "I've got the key in my pocket. Sit down. I want to talk to you. Don't be a fool."

"Where's Bradshaw, Moll?"

"At the depot by this time, I fancy, for the carriage went off at a deuce of a rate."

She laughed again, while he paced the room with angry strides.

"'Twas he, then, that betrayed me. The villain! I'll have his life for that, as I'm a sinner."

"You're a great sinner, Philip Searle. Sit down, now, and be quiet. Where's the girl?"

"What girl?"

"Miranda Ayleff. The girl you've ruined; the girl you've put in my place, and that I've come to drive out of it. Where is she?"

"Don't speak so loud, Moll. Be quiet, can't

you? See here, Moll," he continued, drawing a chair to her side, and speaking in his old winning way—"see here, Moll: why can't you just let this matter stand as it is, and take your share of the plunder? You know I don't care about the girl; so what difference does it make to you, if we allow her to think that she's my lawful wife? Come, give us a kiss, Moll, and let's hear no more about it."

"Honey won't catch such an old fly as I am, Philip," replied the woman, but with a gentler tone. "Where is the girl?" she asked suddenly, starting from the chair. "I want to see her. Is she in there?"

"No," said Philip, quickly, and rising to bar her passage to the door of Miranda's chamber. "She is not there, Moll; you can't see her. Are you crazy? You'd frighten the poor girl out of her senses."

"She's in tnere. I'm going in to speak with her. Yes I shall, Philip, and you needn't stop me."

"Keep back. Keep quiet, can't you?"

"No. Don't hold me, Philip Searle. Keep your hands off me, if you know what's good for you."

She brushed past him, and laid her hand upon the door-knob; but he seized her violently by the arm and pulled her back. The action hurt her wrist, and she was boiling with rage in a second. With her clenched fist, she struck him straight in the face repeatedly, while with every blow, she screamed out an imprecation.

"Keep quiet, you hag! Keep quiet, confound you!" said the infuriated man. "Won't you? Take that!" and he planted his fist upon her mouth.

The woman, through her tears and sobs, howled at him curse upon curse. With one hand upon her throat, he essayed to choke her utterance, and thus they scuffled about the room.

"I'll cut you, Philip; I will, by ——"

Her hand, in fact, was fumbling about her pocket, and she drew forth a small knife and thrust it into his shoulder. They were near the table, over which Philip had thrust her down. He was wild with rage and the brandy he had drank. His right hand instinctively grasped the heavy bottle that by chance it came in contact with. The next instant, it descended full upon her forehead, and with a moan of fear and pain, she fell like lead upon the floor, and lay bleeding and motionless.

Philip, still grasping the shattered bottle, gazed aghast upon the lifeless form. Then a cry of terror burst upon his ear. He turned, and beheld Miranda, with dishevelled hair, pale as her night-clothes, standing at the threshold of the open door. With a convulsive shudder, she staggered into the room, and fainted at his feet, her white arm stained with the blood that was sinking in little pools into the carpet.

He stood there gazing from one to the other, but without seeking to succor either. The fumes of brandy, and the sudden revulsion from active wrath to apathy, seemed to stupefy his brain. At last he stooped beside the outstretched form of Molly, and, with averted face, felt in her pocket and drew out the key. Stealthily, as if he feared that they could hear him, he moved toward the door, opened it, and passing through, closed it gently, as one does who would not waken a sleeping child or invalid. Rapidly, but with soft steps, he descended the stairs, and went out into the darkness and the storm.

CHAPTER XVI.

When Miranda awakened from her swoon, the lamp was burning dimly, and the first light of dawn came faintly through the blinds. All was still around her, and for some moments she could not recall the terrible scene which had passed before her eyes. Presently her fingers came in contact with the clots of gore that were thickening on her garment, and she arose quickly, and, with a shudder, tottered against the wall. Her eyes fell upon Moll's white face, the brow mangled and bruised, and the dishevelled hair soaking in the crimson tide that kept faintly oozing from the cut. She was alone in the house with that terrible object; for Philip, careless of her convenience, had only procured the services of a girl from a neighboring farm-house, who attended to the household duties during the day, and went home in the evening. But her womanly compassion was stronger than her sense of horror, and kneeling by the side of the prostrate woman, with inexpressible relief she perceived, by the slight pulsation of the heart, that life was there. Entering her chamber, she hastily put on a morning wrapper, and returing with towel and water, raised Moll's head upon her lap, and washed the thick blood from her face. The cooling moisture revived the wounded woman; her bosom swelled with a deep sigh, and she opened her eyes and looked languidly around.

"How do you feel now, madam?" asked Miranda, gently.

"Who are you?" said Moll, in reply, after a moment's pause.

"Miranda—Miranda Searle, the wife of Philip," she added, trembling at the remembrance of the woman's treatment at her husband's hands.

Molly raised herself with an effort, and sat upon the floor, looking at Miranda, while she laughed with a loud and hollow sound.

"Philip's wife, eh? And you love him, don't you? Well, dreams can't last forever."

"Don't you feel strong enough to get up and lie upon the bed?" asked Miranda, soothingly, for she was uncomfortable under the strange glare that the woman fixed upon her.

"I'm well enough," said Moll. "Where's Philip?"

"Indeed, I do not know. I am very sorry, ma'am, that—that"——

"Never mind. Give me a glass of water."

Miranda hastened to comply, and Moll swallowed the water, and remained silent for a ment.

"Shan't I go for assistance?" asked Miranda, who was anxious to put an end to this painful interview, and was also distressed about her husband's absence. "There's no one except ourselves in the house, but I can go to the farmer's house near by."

"Not for the world," interrupted Moll, taking her by the arm. "I'm well enough. Here, let me lean on you. That's it. I'll sit on the rocking-chair. Thank you. Just bind my head up, will you? Is it an ugly cut?" she asked, as Miranda, having procured some linen, carefully bandaged the wounded part.

"Oh, yes! It's very bad. Does it pain you much, ma'am?"

"Never mind. There, that will do. Now sit down there. Don't be afraid of me. I ain't a-going to hurt you. It's only the cut that makes me look so ugly."

"Oh, no! I am not at all afraid, ma'am," said Miranda, shuddering in spite of herself.

"You are a sweet-looking girl," said Moll, fixing her haggard, but yet beautiful eyes upon the fragile form beside her. "It's a pity you must be unhappy. Has that fellow been unkind to you?"

"What fellow?" madam.

"Philip."

"He is my husband, madam," replied Miranda, mildly, but with the slightest accent of displeasure.

"He is, eh? Hum! You love him dearly, don't you?"

Miranda blushed, and asked:

"Do you know my husband?"

"Know him! If you knew him as well, it would be better for you. You'll know him well enough before long. You come from Virginia, don't you?"

"Yes."

"You must go back there."

"If Philip wishes it."

"I tell you, you must go at once—to-day. I will give you money, if you have none. And you must never speak of what has happened in this house. Do you understand me?"

"But Philip"——

"Forget Philip. You must never see him any more. Why should you want to? Don't you know that he's a brute, and will beat you as he beat me, if you stay with him. Why should you care about him?"

"He is my husband, and you should not speak about him so to me," said Miranda, struggling with her tears, and scarce knowing in what vein to converse with the rude woman, whose strange language bewildered and frightened her.

"Bah!" said Moll, roughly. "You're a simpleton. There, don't cry, though heaven knows you've cause enough, poor thing! Philip Searle's a villain. I could send him to the State prison if I chose."

"Oh, no! don't say that; indeed, don't."

"I tell you I could; but I will not, if you mind me, and do what I tell you. I'm a bad creature, but I won't harm you, if I can help it. You helped me when I was lying there, after that villain hurt me, and I can't help liking you. And yet you've hurt me, too."

"I!"

"Yes. Shall I tell you a story? Poor girl! you're wretched enough now, but you'd better know the truth at once. Listen to me: I was an innocent girl, like you, once. Not so beautiful, perhaps, and not so good; for I was always proud and willful, and loved to have my own way. I was a country girl, and had money left to me by my dead parents. A young man made my acquaintance. He was gay and handsome, and made me believe that he loved me. Well, I married him—do you hear? I married him—at the church, with witnesses, and a minister to make me his true and lawful wife. Curse him! I wish he had dropped down dead at the altar. There, you needn't shudder; it would have been well for you if he had. I married him, and then commenced my days of sorrow and—of guilt. He squandered my money at the gambling-table, and I was sometimes in rags and without food. He was drunk half the time, and abused me;

but I was even with him there, and gave him as good as he gave me. He taught me to drink, and such a time as we sometimes made together would have made Satan blush. I thought I was low enough; but he drove me lower yet. He put temptation in my way—he did, curse his black heart! though he denied it. I fell as low as woman can fall, and then I suppose you think he left me? Well, he did, for a time; he went off somewhere, and perhaps it was then he was trying to ruin some other girl, as foolish as I had been. But he came back, and got money from me—the wages of my sin. And all the while, he was as handsome, and could talk as softly as if he was a saint. And with that smooth tongue and handsome face he won another bride, and married her—married her, I tell you; and that's why I can send him to the State prison."

"Send him! Who? My God! what do you mean?" cried Miranda, rising slowly from her chair, with clasped hands and ashen cheeks.

"Philip Searle, my husband!" shouted Moll, rising also, and standing with gleaming eyes before the trembling girl.

Miranda sank slowly back into her seat, tear-less, but shuddering as with an ague fit. Only from her lips, with a moaning sound, a murmur came:

"No, no, no! oh, no!"

"May God strike me dead this instant, if it is not true!" said Moll, sadly; for she felt for the poor girl's distress.

Miranda rose, her hands pressed tightly against her heart, and moved toward the door with tottering and uncertain steps, like one who suffocates and seeks fresh air. Then her white lips were stained with purple; a red stream gushed from her mouth and dyed the vestment on her bosom; and ere Moll could reach her, she had sunk, with an agonizing sob, upon the floor.

CHAPTER XVII.

THE night after the unhappy circumstance we have related, in the bar-room of a Broadway hotel, in New York city, a colonel of volunteers, moustached and uniformed, and evidently in a very unmilitary condition of unsteadiness, was entertaining a group of convivial acquaintances, with bacchanalian exercises and martian gossip.

He had already, with a month's experience at the seat of war, culled the glories of unfought fields, and was therefore an object of admiration to his civilian friends, and of envy to several unfledged heroes, whose maiden swords had as yet only jingled on the pavement of Broadway, or flashed in the gaslight of saloons. They were yet none the less conscious of their own importance, these embryo Napoleons, but wore their shoulder straps with a killing air, and had often, on a sunny afternoon, stood the fire of bright eyes from innumerable promenading batteries, with gallantry, to say the least.

And now they stood, like Cæsars, amid clouds of smoke, and wielded their formidable goblets with the ease of veterans, though not always with a soldierly precision. And why should they not? Their tailors had made them heroes, every one; and they had never yet once led the van in a retreat.

"And how's Tim?" asked one of the black-coated hangers-on upon prospective glory.

"Tim's in hot water," answered the colonel, elevating his chin and elbow with a gesture more suggestive of Bacchus than of Mars.

"Hot brandy and water would be more like him," said the acknowledged wit of the party, looking gravely at the sugar in his empty glass, as if indifferent to the bursts of laughter which rewarded his appropriate sally

"I'll tell you about it," said the colonel. "Fill up, boys. Thompson, take a fresh segar."

Thompson took it, and the boys filled up, while the colonel flung down a specimen of Uncle Sam's eagle with an emphasis that demonstrated what he would do for the bird when opportunity offered.

"You see, we had a party of Congressmen in camp, and were cracking some champagne bottles in the adjutant's tent. We considered it a military necessity to floor the legislators, you know; but one old senator was tough as a siege-gun, and wouldn't even wink at his third bottle. So the corks flew about like minié balls, but never a man but was too good a soldier to cry 'hold, enough.' As for that old demijohn of a senator, it seemed he couldn't hold enough, and wouldn't if he could; so we directed the main battle against him, and opened a masked battery upon him, by uncovering a bottle of Otard; but he never flinched. It was a game of *Brag* all over, and every one kept ordering 'a little more grape.' Presently, up slaps a mounted aid, galloping like mad, and in tumbles the sleepy orderly for the officer of the day.

"'That's you, Tim,' says I. But Tim was just then singing the Star Spangled Banner in a convivial whisper to the tune of the Red, White, and Blue, and wouldn't be disturbed on no account.

"'Tumble out, Tim,' says I, 'or I'll have you court-martialled and shot.'

"'In the neck,' says Tim. But he did manage to tumble out, and finished the last stanzas with a flourish, for the edification of the mounted aid-de-camp.

"'Where's the officer of the day?' asked the aid, looking suspiciously at Tim's shaky knees.

"'He stands before you,' replied Tim, steadying himself a little by affectionately hanging on to the horse's tail.

"'You sir? you're unfit for duty, and I'll report you, sir, at headquarters,' said the aid, who was a West Pointer, you know, stiff as a poker in regimentals.

"'Sir!—hic,' replied Tim, with an attempt at offended dignity, the effect of which was rather spoiled by the accompanying hiccough.

"'Where's the colonel!' asked the aid.

"'Drunk,' says that rascal, Tim, confidentially, with a knowing wink.

"'Where's the adjutant?'

"'Drunk.'

"'Good God, sir, are you all drunk?'

"''Cept the surgeon—he's got the measles.'

"'Orderly, give this dispatch to the first sober officer you can find.'

"'It's no use, captain,' says Tim, 'the regiment's drunk—'cept me, hic!' and Tim lost his balance, and tumbled over the orderly, for you see the captain put spurs to his horse rather suddenly, and whisked the friendly tail out of his hands.

"So we were all up before the general the next day, but swore ourselves clear, all except Tim, who had the circumstantial evidence rather too strong against him."

"And such are the men in whom the country has placed its trust?" muttered a grey-headed old gentleman, who, while apparently absorbed in his newspaper, had been listening to the colonel's narrative.

A young man who had lounged into the room approached the party and caught the colonel's eye:

"Ah! Searle, how are you? Come up and take a drink."

A further requisition was made upon the bartender, and the company indulged anew. Searle, although a little pale and nervous, was all life and gaiety. His coming was a fresh brand on the convivial flame, and the party, too much exhilarated to be content with pushing one vice to excess, sallied forth in search of whatever other the great city might afford. They had not to look far. Folly is at no fault in the metropolis for food of whatever quality to feed upon; and they were soon accommodated with excitement to their hearts content at a fashionable gambling saloon on Broadway. The colonel played with recklessness and daring that, if he carries it to the battle-field, will wreathe his brow with laurels; but like many a rash soldier before him, he did not win. On the contrary, his eagles took flight with a rapidity suggestive of the old adage that "gold hath wings," and when, long after midnight, he stood upon the deserted street alone with Philip Searle and his reflections, he was a sadder and a soberer man.

"Searle, I'm a ruined man."

"You'll fight all the better for it," replied Philip, knocking the ashes from his segar. "Come, you'll never mend the matter by taking cold here in the night air; where do you put up? I'll see you home."

"D—n you, you take it easy," said the colonel, bitterly. Philip could afford to take it easy, for he had most of the colonel's money in his pocket. In fact, the unhappy votary of Mars was more thoroughly ruined than his companion was aware of, for when fortune was hitting him hardest, he had not hesitated to bring into action a reserve of government funds which had been intrusted to his charge for specific purposes.

"Searle," said the colonel, after they had walked along silently for a few minutes, "I was telling you this evening about that vacant captaincy."

"Yes, you were telling me I shouldn't have it," replied Philip, with an accent of injured friendship.

"Well, I fancied it out of my power to do anything about it. But"——

"Well, but?"——

"I think I might get it for you, for—for"——

"A consideration?" suggested Philip, interrogatively.

Well, to be plain with you, let me have five

hundred, and you've won all of that to-night, and I'll get you the captaincy."

"We'll talk about it to-morrow morning," replied Philip.

And in the morning the bargain was concluded; Philip, with the promise that all should be satisfactorily arranged, started the same day for Washington, to await the commission so honorably disposed of by the gallant colonel.

CHAPTER XVIII.

We will let thirty days pass on, and bear the reader South of the Potomac, beyond the Federal lines and within rifle-shot of an advanced picket of the Confederate army, under General Beauregard. It was a dismal night—the 16th of July. The rain fell heavily and the wind moaned and shrieked through the lone forests like unhappy spirits wailing in the darkness. A solitary horseman was cautiously wending his way through the storm upon the Centreville road and toward the Confederate line. He bore a white handkerchief, and from time to time, as his ear seemed to catch a sound other than the voice of the tempest, he drew his rein and raised the fluttering symbol at his drawn sword's point. Through the dark masses of foliage that skirted the roadside, presently could be seen the fitful glimmer of a watchfire, and the traveller redoubled his precautions, but yet rode steadily on.

"Halt!" cried a stern, loud voice from a clump of bushes that looked black and threatening in the darkness. The horseman checked his horse and sat immovable in the centre of the road.

"Who goes there?" followed quick, in the same deep, peremptory tone.

"An officer of the United States, with a flag of truce," was answered in a clear, firm voice.

"Stand where you are." There was a pause, and presently four dark forms emerged from the roadside, and stood at the horse's head.

"You've chosen a strange time for your errand, and a dangerous one," said one of the party, with a mild and gentlemanly accent.

"Who speaks?"

"The officer in command of this picket."

"Is not that Beverly Weems?"

"The same. And surely I know that voice."

"Of course you do, if you know Harold Hare."

And the stranger, dismounting, stretched out his hand, which was eagerly and warmly clasped, and followed by a silent and prolonged embrace.

"How rash you have been, Harold," said Beverly, at last. "It is a mercy that I was by, else might a bullet have been your welcome. Why did you not wait till morning?"

"Because my mission admits of no delay. It is most opportune that I have met you. You have spoken to me at times, and Oriana often, of your young cousin, Miranda."

"Yes, Harold, what of her?"

"Beverly, she is within a rifle-shot of where we stand, very sick—dying I believe."

"Good God, Harold! what strange tale is this?"

"I am in command of an advanced picket, stationed at the old farm-house yonder. Toward dusk this evening, a carriage drove up, and when challenged, a pass was presented, with orders to assist the bearer, Miranda Ayleff, beyond the lines. I remembered the name, and stepping to the carriage door, beheld two females, one of whom was bending over her companion, and holding a vial, a restorative, I suppose, to her lips.

"'She has fainted, sir,' said the woman, 'and is very ill. I'm afraid she won't last till she gets to Richmond. Can't you help her; isn't there a surgeon among you at the farm-house there?'

"We had no surgeon, but I had her taken into the house, and made as comfortable as possible. When she recovered from her swoon, she asked for you, and repeatedly for Oriana, and would not be comforted until I promised her that she should be taken immediately on to Richmond. 'She could not die there, among strangers,' she said; 'she must see one friend before she died. She must go home at once and be forgiven.' And thus she went, half in delirium, until I feared that her life would pass away, from sheer exhaustion. I determined to ride over to your picket at once, not dreaming, however, that you were in command. At dawn to-morrow we shall probably be relieved, and it might be beyond my power then to meet her wishes."

"I need not say how much I thank you, Harold. But you were ever kind and generous. Poor girl! Let us ride over at once, Harold. Who is her companion?"

"A woman some years her senior, but yet young, though prematurely faded. I could get little from her. Not even her name. She is gloomy and reserved, even morose at times; but she seems to be kind and attentive to Miranda."

Beverly left some hasty instructions with his sergeant, and rode over with Harold to the farm-house. They found Miranda reclining upon a couch of blankets, over which Harold had spread his military cloak, for the dwelling had been stripped of its furniture, and was, in fact, little more than a deserted ruin. The suffering girl was pale and attenuated, and her sunken eyes were wild and bright with the fire of delirium. Yet she seemed to recognize Beverly, and stretched out her thin arms when he approached, exclaiming in tremulous accents:

"Take me home, Beverly, oh, take me home!"

Moll was seated by her side, upon a soldier's knapsack; her chin resting upon her hands, and her black eyes fixed sullenly upon the floor. She would give but short and evasive answers to Beverly's questions, and stubbornly refused to communicate the particulars of Miranda's history.

"She broke a blood-vessel a month ago in

Boston. But she got better, and was always wanting to go to her friends in Richmond. And so I brought her on. And now you must take care of her, for I'm going back to camp."

This was about all the information she would give, and the two young men ceased to importune her, and directed their attentions to the patient.

The carriage was prepared and the cushions so arranged, with the help of blankets, as to form a kind of couch within the vehicle. Upon this Miranda was tenderly lifted, and when she was told that she should be taken home without delay, and would soon see Oriana, she smiled like a pleased child, and ceased complaining.

Beverly stood beside his horse, with his hand clasped in Harold's. The rain poured down upon them, and the single watchfire, a little apart from which the silent sentinel stood leaning on his rifle, threw its rude glare upon their saddened faces.

"Good bye, old friend," said Beverly. "We have met strangely to-night, and sadly. Pray heaven we may not meet more sadly on the battle-field."

"Tell Oriana," replied Harold, "that I am with her in my prayers." He had not spoken of her before, although Beverly had mentioned that she was at the old manor house, and well. "I have not heard from Arthur," he continued, "for I have been much about upon scouting parties since I came, but I doubt not he is well, and I may find a letter when I return to camp. Good bye; and may our next meeting see peace upon the land."

They parted, and the carriage, with Beverly riding at its side, moved slowly into the darkness, and was gone.

Harold returned into the farm-house, and found Moll seated where he had left her, and still gazing fixedly at the floor. He did not disturb her, but paced the floor slowly, lost in his own melancholy thoughts. After a silence of some minutes, the woman spoke, without looking up.

"Have they gone?"

"Yes."

"She is dying, ain't she?"

"I fear she is very ill."

"I tell you, she's dying—and it's better that she is."

She then relapsed into her former mood, but after a while, as Harold paused at the window and looked out, she spoke again.

"Will it soon be day?"

"Within an hour, I think," replied Harold. "Do you go back at daylight?"

"Yes."

"You have no horse?"

"You'll lend me one, won't you? If you don't, I don't care; I can walk."

"We will do what we can for you. What is your business at the camp?"

"Never mind," she answered gruffly. And then, after a pause, she asked:

"Is there a man named Searle in your army —Philip Searle?"

"Nay, I know not. There may be. I have never heard the name. Do you seek such a person? Is he your friend, or relative?"

"Never mind," she said again, and then was silent as before.

With the approach of dawn, the sentry challenged an advancing troop, which proved to be the relief picket guard. Harold saluted the officer in command, and having left orders respectively with their subordinates, they entered the farm-house together, and proceeded to the apartment where Moll still remained seated. She did not seem to notice their entrance; but when the new-comer's voice, in some casual remark, reached her ear, she rose up suddenly, and walking straight forward to where the two stood, looking out at the window, she placed her hand heavily, and even rudely, upon his shoulder. He turned at the touch, and beholding her, started back, with not only astonishment, but fear.

"You needn't look so white, Philip Searle," she said at last, in a low, hoarse tone. "It's not a ghost you're looking at. But perhaps you're only angry that you only half did your business while you were at it."

"Where did you pick up this woman?" asked Searle of Harold, drawing him aside.

"She came with an invalid on her way to Richmond," replied Harold.

"What invalid?"

He spoke almost in a whisper, but Moll overheard him, and answered fiercely:

"One that is dying, Philip; and you know

well enough who murdered her. 'Twasn't me you struck the hardest blow that night. Do you see that scar? That's nothing; but you struck her to the heart."

"What does she mean?" asked Harold, looking sternly into Philip's disturbed eye.

"Heaven knows. She's mad," he answered. "Did she tell you nothing—no absurd story?"

"Nothing. She was sullen and uncommunicative, and half the time took no notice of our questions."

"No wonder, poor thing!" said Philip. "She's mad. However, I have some little power with her, and if you will leave us alone awhile, I will prevail upon her to go quietly back to Washington."

Harold went up to the woman, who was leaning with folded arms against the wall, and spoke kindly to her.

"Should you want assistance, I will help you. We shall be going in half an hour. You must be ready to go with us, you know, for you can't stay here, where there may be fighting presently."

"Thank you," she replied. "Don't mind me.

I can take care of myself. You can leave us alone together. I'm not afraid of him."

Harold left the room, and busied himself about the preparations for departure. Left alone with the woman he had wronged, Philip for some moments paced the room nervously and with clouded brow. Finally, he stopped abruptly before Moll, who had been following his motions with her wild, unquiet eyes.

"Where have you sprung from now, and what do you want?"

"Do you see that scar?" she said again, but more fiercely than before. "While that lasts, there's no love 'twixt you and me, and it'll last me till my death."

"Then why do you trouble me. If you don't love me, why do you hang about me wherever I go? We'll be better friends away from each other than together. Why don't you leave me alone?"

"Ha! ha! we must be quits for that, you know," she answered, rather wildly, and pointing to her forehead. "Do you think I'm a poor whining fool like her, to get sick and die when you abuse me? I'll haunt you till I die, Philip;

and after, too, if I can, to punish you for that."

Philip fancied that he detected the gleam of insanity in her eye, and he was not wrong, for the terrible blow he had inflicted had injured her brain; and her mind, weakened by dissipation and the action of excitement upon her violent temperament, was tottering upon the verge of madness.

"When I was watching that poor sick girl," she continued, "I thought I could have loved her, she was so beautiful and gentle, as she lay there, white and thin, and never speaking a word against you, Philip, but thinking of her friends far away, and asking to be taken home—home, where her mother was sleeping under the sod— home, to be loved and kissed again before she died. And I would have loved her if I hadn't hated you so much that there wasn't room for the love of any living creature in my bad heart. I used to sit all night and hear her talk—talk in her dreams and in her fever—as if there were kind people listening to her, people that were kind to her long ago. And the room seemed full of angels sometimes, so that I was afraid to move and look about; for I could swear I heard the fanning of their wings and the rustle of their feet upon the carpet. Sometimes I saw big round tears upon her wasted cheeks, and I wouldn't brush them away, for they looked like jewels that the angels had dropped there. And then I tried to cry myself, but, ha! ha! I had to laugh instead, although my heart was bursting. I wished I could have cried; I'm sure it would have made my heart so light, and perhaps it would have burst that ring of hot iron that was pressing so hard around my head. It's there now, sinking and burning right against my temples. But I can't cry, I haven't since I was a little girl, long ago, long ago; but I think I cried when mother died, long ago, long ago."

She was speaking in a kind of dreamy murmur, while Philip paced the room; and finally she sank down upon the floor, and sat there with her hands pressed against her brows, rocking herself to and fro.

"Moll," said Philip, stooping over her, and speaking in a gentle tone, "I'm sorry I struck you, indeed I am; but I was drunk, and when you cut me, I didn't know what I was about.

Now let's be friends, there's a good girl. You must go back to Washington, you know, and to New York, and stay there till I come back. Won't you, now, Moll?"

"Won't I? No, Philip Searle, I won't. I'll stay by you till you kill me; yes, I will. You want to go after that poor girl and torment her; but she's dying and soon you won't be able to hurt her any more."

"Was it she, Moll, was it Miranda that came here with you? Was she going to Richmond?"

"She was going to heaven, Philip Searle, out of the reach of such as you and me. I'm good enough for you, Philip, bad as I am; and I'm your wife, besides."

"You told her that?"

"Told her? Ha! ha! Told her? do you think I'm going to make that a secret? No, no. We're a bad couple, sure enough; but I'm not going to deny you, for all that. Look you, young man," she continued, addressing Harold, who at that moment entered the room, "that is Philip Searle, and Philip Searle is my husband— my husband, curse his black heart! and if he dares deny it, I'll have him in the State prison, for I can do it."

"She's perfectly insane," said Philip; but Harold looked thoughtful and perplexed, and scanned his fellow-officer's countenance with a searching glance.

"At all events," he said, "she must not remain here. My good woman, we are ready now, and you must come with us. We have a horse for you, and will make you comfortable. Are you ready?"

"No," she replied, sullenly, "I won't go. I'll stay with my husband."

"Nay," remonstrated Harold, gently, "you cannot stay here. This is no place for women. When we arrive at headquarters, you shall tell your story to General McDowell, and he will see that you are taken care of, and have justice if you have been wronged. But you must not keep us waiting. We are soldiers, you know, and must do our duty."

Still, however, she insisted upon remaining where she was; but when two soldiers, at a gesture from Harold, approached and took her gently by the arms, she offered no resistance, and suffered herself to be led quietly out. Harold coldly saluted Searle, and left him in charge of the post; while himself and party, accompanied by Moll and the coachman who had driven them from Washington, were soon briskly marching toward the camp.

CHAPTER XIX.

Toward dusk of the same day, while Philip and his lieutenant were seated at the rude pine table, conversing after their evening meal, the sergeant of the guard entered with a slip of paper, on which was traced a line in pencil.

"Is the bearer below?" asked Philip, as he cast his eyes over the paper.

"Yes, sir. He was challenged a minute ago, and answered with the countersign and that slip for you, sir."

"It's all right, sergeant; you may send him up. Mr. Williams," he continued, to his comrade, "will you please to look about a little and see that all is in order. I will speak a few words with this messenger."

The lieutenant and sergeant left the room, and presently afterward there entered, closing the door carefully after him, no less a personage than Seth Rawbon.

"You're late," said Philip, motioning him to a chair.

"There's an old proverb to answer that," answered Rawbon, as he leisurely adjusted his lank frame upon the seat. Having established himself to his satisfaction, he continued:

"I had to make a considerable circuit to avoid the returning picket, who might have bothered me with questions. I'm in good time, though. If you've made up your mind to go, you'll do it as well by night, and safer too."

"What have you learned?"

"Enough to make me welcome at headquarters. You were right about the battle. There'll be tough work soon. They're fixing for a general advance. If you expect to do your first fighting under the stars and bars, you must swear by them to-night."

"Have you been in Washington?"

"Every nook and corner of it. They don't keep their eyes skinned, I fancy, up there. Your fancy colonels have slippery tongues when the champagne corks are flying. If they fight as hard as they drink, they'll give us trouble. Well, what do you calculate to do?" he added, after a pause, during which Philip was moody and lost in thought.

Philip rose from his seat and paced the floor uneasily, while Rawbon filled a glass from a flask of brandy on the table. It was now quite dark without, and neither of them observed the figure of a woman crouched on the narrow veranda, her chin resting on the sill of the open window. At last Philip resumed his seat, and he, too, swallowed a deep draught from the flask of brandy.

"Tell me what I can count upon?" he asked.

"The same grade you have, and in a crack regiment. It's no use asking for money. They've none to spare for such as you—now don't look savage—I mean they won't buy men that hain't seen service, and you can't expect them to. I told you all about that before, and it's time you had your mind made up."

"What proofs of good faith can you give me?"

Rawbon thrust his hand into his bosom and drew out a roll of parchment.

"This commission, under Gen. Beauregard's hand, to be approved when you report yourself at headquarters."

Philip took the document and read it attentively, while Rawbon occupied himself with filling his pipe from a leathern pouch. The female figure stepped in at the window, and, gliding noiselessly into the room, seated herself in a third chair by the table before either of the men became aware of her presence. They started up with astonishment and consternation. She did not seem to heed them, but leaning upon the table, she stretched her hand to the brandy flask and applied it to her lips.

"Who's this?" demanded Rawbon, with his hand upon the hilt of his large bowie knife.

"Curse her! my evil genius," answered Philip, grating his teeth with anger. It was Moll.

"What's this, Philip!" she said, clutching the parchment which had been dropped upon the table.

"Leave that," ejaculated her husband, savagely, and darting to take it from her

But she eluded his grasp, and ran with the document into a corner of the room.

"Ha! ha! ha! I know what it is," she said, waving it about as a schoolboy sometimes exultingly exhibits a toy that he has mischievously snatched from a comrade.

"It's your death-warrant, Philip Searle, if somebody sees it over yonder. I heard you. I heard you. You're going over to fight for Jeff. Davis. Well, I don't care, but I'll go with you. Don't come near me. Don't hurt me, Philip, or I'll scream to the soldier out there."

"I won't hurt you, Moll. Be quiet now, there's a good girl. Come here and take a sup more of brandy."

"I won't. You want to hurt me. But you can't. I'm a match for you both. Ha! ha! You don't know how nicely I slipped away from the soldiers when they were resting. I went into the thick bushes, right down in the water, and lay still. I wanted to laugh when I saw them hunting for me, and I could almost have touched the young officer if I had wished. But I lay still as a mouse, and they went off and never found me. Ha! ha! ha!"

"Is she drunk or mad?" asked Rawbon.

"Mad," answered Philip, "but cunning enough to do mischief, if she has a mind to. Moll, dear, come sit down here and be quiet; come, now."

"Mad? mad?" murmured Moll, catching his word. "No, I'm not mad," she continued wildly, passing her hands over her brows, "but I saw spirits just now in the woods, and heard voices, and they've frightened me. The ghost of the girl that died in the hospital was there. You knew little blue-eyed Lizzie, Philip. She was cursing me when she died and calling for her mother. But I don't care. The man paid me well for getting her, and 'twasn't my fault if she got sick and died. Poor thing! poor thing! poor little blue-eyed Lizzie! She was innocent enough when she first came, but she got to be as bad as any—until she got sick and died. Poor little Lizzie!" And thus murmuring incoherently, the unhappy woman sat down upon the floor, and bent her head upon her knees.

"Clap that into her mouth," whispered Philip, handing Rawbon his handkerchief rolled tightly into a ball. "Quietly now, but quick. Look out now. She's strong as a trooper."

They approached her without noise, but suddenly, and while Philip grasped her wrists, Rawbon threw back her head, and forcing the jaws open by a violent pressure of his knuckles against the joint, thrust the handkerchief between her teeth and bound it tightly there with two turns of his sash. The shriek was checked upon her lips and changed into a painful, gurgling groan. The poor creature, with convulsive efforts, struggled to free her arms from Philip's grasp, but he managed to keep his hold until Rawbon had secured her wrists with the stout cord that suspended his canteen. A silk neckerchief was then tightly bound around her ankles, and Moll, with heaving breast and glaring eyes, lay, moaning piteously, but speechless and motionless, upon the floor.

"We can leave her there," said Rawbon. "It's not likely any of your men will come in, until morning at least. Let's be off at once."

Philip snatched up the parchment where it had fallen, and silently followed his companion.

"We are going beyond the line to look about a bit," he said to the sergeant on duty, as they passed his post. "Keep all still and quiet till we return."

"Take some of the boys with you, captain," replied the sergeant. "We're unpleasant close to those devils, sir."

"It's all right, sergeant. There's no danger." And nodding to Seth, the two walked leisurely along the road until concealed by the darkness, when they quickened their pace and pushed boldly toward the Confederate lines.

Half an hour, or less perhaps, after their departure, the sentry, posted at about a hundred yards from the house, observed an unusual light gleaming from the windows of the old farm-house. He called the attention of Lieutenant Williams, who was walking by in conversation with the sergeant, to the circumstance.

"Is not the captain there?" asked the lieutenant.

"No, sir," replied the sergeant, "he started off to go beyond the line half an hour ago."

"Alone?"

"No, sir; that chap that came in at dusk was with him."

"It's strange he should have gone without speaking to me about it."

"I wanted him to take some of our fellows along, sir, but he didn't care to. By George! that house is afire, sir. Look there."

While talking, they had been proceeding

toward the farm-house, when the light from the windows brightened suddenly into a broad glare, and called forth the sergeant's exclamation. Before they reached the building a jet of flame had leaped from one of the casements, and continued to whirl like a flaming ribbon in the air. They quickened their pace to a run, and bursting into the doorway, were driven back by a dense volume of smoke, that rolled in black masses along the corridor. They went in again, and the sergeant pushed open the door of the room where Moll lay bound, but shut it quickly again, as a tongue of flame lashed itself toward him like an angry snake.

"It's all afire, sir," he said, coughing and spluttering through the smoke. "Are there any of the captain's traps inside?"

"Nothing at all," replied the lieutenant. "Let's go in, however, and see what can be done."

They entered, but were driven back by the baffling smoke and the flames that were now licking all over the dry plastering of the room.

"It's no use," said the lieutenant, when they had gained their breath in the open air.

"There's no water, except in the brook down yonder, and what the men have in their canteens. The house is like tinder. Let it go, sergeant; it's not worth saving at the risk of singing your whiskers."

The men had now come up, and gathered about the officer to receive his commands.

"Let the old shed go, my lads," he said. "It's well enough that some rebel should give us a bonfire now and then. Only stand out of the glare, boys, or you may have some of those devils yonder making targets of you."

The men fell back into the shadow, and standing in little groups, or seated upon the sward, watched the burning house, well pleased to have some spectacle to relieve the monotony of the night. And they looked with indolent gratification, passing the light jest and the merry word, while the red flames kept up their wild sport, and great masses of rolling vapor upheaved from the crackling roof, and blackened the midnight sky. None sought to read the mystery of that conflagration. It was but an old barn gone to ashes a little before its time. Perhaps some mischievous hand among them had applied the torch for a bit of deviltry. Perhaps the flames had caught from Rawbon's pipe, which he had thrown carelessly among a heap of rubbish when startled by Molly's sudden apparition. Or yet, perhaps, though Heaven forbid it, for the sake of human nature, the same hand that had struck so nearly fatally once, had been tempted to complete the work of death in a more terrible form.

But within those blistering walls, who can tell what ghastly revels the mad flames were having over their bound and solitary victim! Perhaps, as she lay there with distended jaws, and eyeballs starting from their sockets, that brain, amid the visions of its madness, became conscious of the first kindling of the subtle element that was so soon to clasp her in its terrible embrace. How dreadful, while the long minutes dragged, to watch its stealthy progress, and to feel that one little effort of an unbound hand could avert the danger, and yet to lie there helpless, motionless, without even the power to give utterance to the shriek of terror which strained her throat to suffocation. And then, as the creeping flame became stronger and brighter, and took long and silent leaps from one object to another, gliding along the lathed and papered wall, rolling and curling along the raftered ceiling, would not the wretched woman, raving already in delirium, behold the spectres that her madness feared, beckoning to her in the lurid glare, or gliding in and out among the wild fires that whirled in fantastic gambols around and overhead! Nearer and nearer yet the rolling flame advances; it commences to hiss and murmur in its progress; it wreathes itself about the chairs and tables, and laps up the little pool of brandy spilled from the forgotten flask; it plays about her feet, and creeps lazily amid the folds of her gown, yet wet from the brook in which she had concealed herself that day; it scorches and shrivels up the flesh upon her limbs, while pendent fiery tongues leap from the burning rafters, and kiss her cheeks and brows where the black veins swell almost to bursting; every muscle and nerve of her frame is strained with convulsive efforts to escape, but the cords only sink into the bloating flesh, and she lies there crisping like a log, and as powerless to move.

The dense, black smoke hangs over her like a pall, but prostrate as she is, it cannot sink low enough to suffocate and end her agony. How the bared bosom heaves! how the tortured limbs writhe, and the blackening cuticle emits a nauseous steam! The black blood oozing from her nostrils proclaims how terrible the inward struggle. The whole frame bends and shrinks, and warps like a fragment of leather thrown into a furnace—the flame has reached her vitals—at last, by God's mercy, she is dead.

CHAPTER XX.

At dawn of the morning of the 21st of July, an officer in plain undress was busily writing at a table in a plainly-furnished apartment of a farm-house near Manassas. He was of middle age and medium size, with dark complexion, bold, prominent features, and steady, piercing black eyes. His manner and the respectful demeanor of several officers in attendance, rather than any insignia of office which he wore, bespoke him of high rank; and the earnest attention which he bestowed upon his labor, together with the numerous orders, written and verbal, which he delivered at intervals to members of his staff, denoted that an affair of importance was in hand. Several horses, ready caparisoned, were held by orderlies at the doorway, and each aid, as he received instructions, mounted and dashed away at a gallop.

The building was upon a slight elevation of land, and along the plain beneath could be seen the long rows of tents and the curling smoke of camp-fires; while the hum of many voices in the distance, with here and there a bugle-blast and the spirit-stirring roll of drums, denoted the site of the Confederate army. The reveille had just sounded, and the din of active preparation could be heard throughout the camp. Regiments were forming, and troops of horse were marshalling in squadron, while others were galloping here and there; while, through the ringing of sabres and the strains of marshal music, the low rumbling of the heavy-wheeled artillery was the most ominous sound.

An orderly entered the apartment where General Beauregard was writing, and spoke with one of the members of the staff in waiting.

"What is it, colonel?" asked the general, looking up.

"An officer from the outposts, with two prisoners, general." And he added something in a lower tone.

"Very opportune," said Beauregard. "Let them come in."

The orderly withdrew and reëntered with Captain Weems, followed by Philip Searle and

Rawbon. A glance of recognition passed between the latter and Beauregard, and Seth, obeying a gesture of the general, advanced and placed a small package on the table. The general opened it hastily and glanced over its contents.

"As I thought," he muttered. "You are sure as to the disposition of the advance?"

"Quite sure of the main features."

"When did you get in?"

"Only an hour ago. Their vanguard was close behind. Before noon, I think they will be upon you in three columns from the different roads."

"Very well, you may go now. Come to me in half an hour. I shall have work for you. Who is that with you?"

"Captain Searle."

"Of whom we spoke?"

"The same."

The general nodded, and Seth left the apartment. Beauregard for a second scanned Philip's countenance with a searching glance.

"Approach, sir, if you please. We have little time for words. Have you information to impart?"

"Nothing beyond what I think you know already. You may expect at every moment to hear the boom of McDowell's guns."

"On the right?"

"I think the movement will be on your left. Richardson remains on the southern road, in reserve. Tyler commands the centre. Carlisle, Ricket and Ayre will give you trouble there with their batteries. Hunter and Heintzelman, with fourteen thousand, will act upon your left."

"Then we are wrong, Taylor," said Beauregard, turning to an officer at his side; and rising, the two conversed for a moment in low but earnest tone.

"It is plausible," said Beauregard, at length. "Taylor, ride down to Bee and see about it. Captain Searle, you will report yourself to Colonel Hampton at once. He will have orders for you. Captain Weems, you will please see him provided for. Come, gentlemen, to the field!"

The general and his staff were soon mounted and riding rapidly toward the masses and long lines of troops that were marshalling on the plain below.

Beverly stood at the doorway alone with

Philip Searle. He was grave and sad, although the bustle and preparation of an expected battle lent a lustre to his eye. To his companion he was stern and distant, and they both walked onward for some moments without a word. At a short distance from the building, they came upon a black groom holding two saddled horses.

"Mount, sir, if you please," said Beverly, and they rode forward at a rapid pace. Philip was somewhat surprised to observe that their course lay away from the camp, and in fact the sounds of military life were lessening as they went on. They passed the brow of the hill and descended by a bridle-path into a little valley, thick with shrubbery and trees. At the gateway of a pleasant looking cottage Beverly drew rein.

"I must ask you to enter here," he said, dismounting. "Within a few hours we shall both be, probably, in the ranks of battle; but first I have a duty to perform."

They entered the cottage, within which all was hushed and still; the sounds of an active household were not heard. They ascended the little stair, and Beverly pushed gently open the door of an apartment and motioned to Philip to enter. He paused at first, for as he stood on the threshold a low sob reached his ear.

"Pass in," said Beverly, in a grave, stern tone. "I have promised that I would bring you, else, be assured, I would not linger in your presence."

They entered. It was a small, pleasant room, and through the lattice interwoven with woodbine the rising sun looked in like a friendly visitor. Upon a bed was stretched the form of a young girl, sleeping or dead, it would be hard to tell, the features were so placid and beautiful in repose. One ray of sunlight fell among the tangles of her golden hair, and glowed like a halo above the marble-white brow. The long dark lashes rested upon her cheek with a delicate contrast like that of the velvety moss when it peeps from the new-fallen snow. Her hands were folded upon her bosom above the white coverlet; they clasped a lily, that seemed as if sculptured upon a churchyard stone, so white was the flower, so white the bosom that it pressed. One step nearer revealed that she was dead; earthly sleep was never so calm and beautiful. By the bedside Oriana Weems was seated, weeping silently. She arose when her brother entered, and went to him, putting her hands about his neck. Beverly tenderly circled his arm about her waist, and they stood together at the bedside, gazing on all that death had left upon earth of their young cousin, Miranda.

"She died this morning very soon after you left," said Oriana, "without pain and I think without sorrow, for she wore that same sweet smile that you see now frozen upon her lips. Oh, Beverly, I am sorry you brought *him* here!" she added, in a lower tone, glancing with a shudder at Philip Searle, who stood looking with a frown out at the lattice, and stopping the sunbeam from coming into the room. "It seems," she continued, "as if his presence brought a curse that would drag upon the angels' wings that are bearing her to heaven. Though, thank God, she is beyond his power to harm her now!" and she knelt beside the pillow and pressed her lips upon the cold, white brow.

"She wished to see him, Oriana, before she died," said Beverly, "and I promised to bring him; and yet I am glad she passed away before his coming, for I am sure he could bring no peace with him for the dying, and his presence now is but an insult to the dead."

When he had spoken, there was silence for a while, which was broken by the sudden boom of a distant cannon. They all started at the sound, for it awakened them from mournful memories, to yet perhaps more solemn thoughts of what was to come before that bright sun should rise upon the morrow. Beverly turned slowly to where Philip stood, and pointed sternly at the death-bed.

"You have seen enough, if you have dared to look at all," he said. "I have not the power, nor the will, to punish. A soldier's death to-day is what you can best pray for, that you may not live to think of this hereafter. She sent for you to forgive you, but died and you are unforgiven. Bad as you are, I pity you that you must go to battle haunted by the remembrance of this murder that you have done."

Philip half turned with an angry curl upon his lip, as if prepared for some harsh answer; but he saw the white thin face and folded hands, and left the room without a word.

"Farewell! dear sister," said Beverly, clasping the weeping girl in his arms. "I have already overstaid the hour, and must spur hard to be at my post in time. God bless you! it may be I shall never see you again; if so, I leave you to God and my country. But I trust all will be well."

"Oh, Beverly! come back to me, my brother; I am alone in the world without you. I would not have you swerve from your duty, although death came with it; but yet, remember that I am alone without you, and be not rash or reckless. I will watch and pray for you beside this death-bed, Beverly, while you are fighting, and may God be with you."

Beverly summoned an old negress to the room, and consigned his sister to her care. Descending the stairs rapidly, he leaped upon his horse, and waving his hand to Philip, who was already mounted, they plunged along the valley, and ascending the crest of the hill, beheld, while they still spurred on, the vast army in motion before them, while far off in the vanward, from time to time, the dull, heavy booming of artillery told that the work was already begun.

CHAPTER XXI.

On the evening of the 20th July, Hunter's division, to which Harold Hare was attached, was bivouacked on the old Braddock Road, about a mile and a half southeast of Centreville. It was midnight. There was a strange and solemn hush throughout the camp, broken only by the hail of the sentinel and the occasional trampling of horses hoofs, as some aid-de-camp galloped hastily along the line. Some of the troops were sleeping, dreaming, perhaps, of home, and far away, for the time, from the thought of the morrow's danger. But most were keeping vigil through the long hours of darkness, communing with themselves or talking in low murmurs with some comrade; for each soldier knew that the battle-hour was at hand. Harold was stretched upon his cloak, striving in vain to win the boon of an hour's sleep, for he was weary with the toil of the preceding day; but he could not shut out from his brain the whirl of excitement and suspense which that night kept so many tired fellows wakeful when they most needed rest. It was useless to court slumber, on the eve, perhaps, of his eternal sleep; he arose and walked about into the night. .

Standing beside the dying embers of a watch-fire, wrapped in his blanket, and gazing thoughtfully into the little drowsy flames that yet curled about the blackened fagots, was a tall and manly form, which Harold recognized as that of his companion in arms, a young lieutenant of his company. He approached, and placed his hand upon his fellow-soldier's arm.

"What book of fate are you reading in the ashes, Harry?" he asked, in a pleasant tone, anxious to dispel some portion of his own and his comrade's moodiness.

The soldier turned to him and smiled, but sorrowfully and with effort.

"My own destiny, perhaps," he answered. "Those ashes were glowing once with light and warmth, and before the dawn they will be cold, as you or I may be to-morrow, Harold."

"I thought you were too old a soldier to nurse

such fancies upon the eve of battle. I must confess that I, who am a novice in this work, am as restless and nervous as a woman; but you have been seasoned by a Mexican campaign, and I came to you expressly to be laughed into fortitude again."

"You must go on till you meet one more lighthearted than myself," answered the other, with a sigh. "Ah! Harold, I have none of the old elasticity about me to-night. I would I were back under my father's roof, never to hear the roll of the battle-drum again. This is a cruel war, Harold."

"A just one."

"Yes, but cruel. Have you any that you love over yonder, Harold? Any that are dear to you, and that you must strike at on the morrow?"

"Yes, Harry, that is it. It is, as you say, a cruel war."

"I have a brother there," continued his companion; and he looked sadly into the gloom, as if he yearned through the darkness and distance to catch a glimpse of the well-known form. "A brother that, when I last saw him, was a little rosy-cheeked boy, and used to ride upon my knee. He is scarce more than a boy now, and yet he will shoulder his musket to-morrow, and stand in the ranks perhaps to be cut down by the hand that has caressed him. He was our mother's darling, and it is a mercy that she is not living to see us armed against each other."

"It is a painful thought," said Harold, "and one that you should dismiss from contemplation. The chances are thousands to one that you will never meet in battle."

"I trust the first bullet that will be fired may reach my heart, rather than that we should. But who can tell? I have a strange, gloomy feeling upon me; I would say a presentiment, if I were superstitious."

"It is a natural feeling upon the eve of battle. Think no more of it. Look how prettily the moon is creeping from under the edge of yonder cloud. We shall have a bright day for the fight, I think."

"Yes, that's a comfort. One fights all the better in the warm sunlight, as if to show the bright heavens what bloodthirsty devils we can be upon occasion. Hark!"

It was the roll of the drum, startling the stillness of the night; and presently, the brief, stern orders of the sergeants could be heard calling the men into the ranks. There is a strange mingled feeling of awe and excitement in this marshalling of men at night for a dangerous expedition. The orders are given instinctively in a more subdued and sterner tone, as if in unison with the solemnity of the hour. The tramp of marching feet strikes with a more distinct and hollow sound upon the ear. The dark masses seem to move more compactly, as if each soldier drew nearer to his comrade for companionship. The very horses, although alert and eager, seem to forego their prancing, and move with sober tread. And when the word "forward!" rings along the dark column, and the long and silent ranks bend and move on as with an electric impulse, there is a thrill in every vein, and each heart contracts for an instant, as if the black portals of a terrible destiny were open in the van.

A half hour of silent hurry and activity passed away, and at last the whole army was in motion. It was now three o'clock; the moon shone down upon the serried ranks, gleaming from bayonet and cannon, and stretching long black shadows athwart the road. From time to time along the column could be heard the ringing voice of some commander, as he galloped to the van, cheering his men with some well-timed allusion, or dispelling the surrounding gloom with a cheerful promise of victory. Where the wood road branched from the Warrentown turnpike, Gen. McDowell, standing in his open carriage, looked down upon the passing columns, and raised his hat, when the excited soldiers cheered as they hurried on. Here Hunter's column turned to the right, while the main body moved straight on to the centre. Then all became more silent than before, and the light jest passing from comrade to comrade was less frequent, for each one felt that every step onward brought him nearer to the foe.

The eastern sky soon paled into a greyish light, and ruddy streaks pushed out from the horizon. The air breathed fresher and purer than in the darkness, and the bright sun, with an advance guard of thin, rosy clouds, shot upward from the horizon in a blaze of splendor. It was the Sabbath morn.

The boom of a heavy gun is heard from the centre. Carlisle has opened the ball. The day's work is begun. Another! The echoes spring from the hillsides all around, like a thousand angry tongues that threaten death. But on the right, no trace of an enemy is to be seen. Burnside's brigade was in the van; they reached the ford at Sudley's Springs; a momentary confusion ensues as the column prepares to cross. Soon the men are pushing boldly through the shallow stream, but the temptation is too great for their parched throats; they stoop to drink and to fill their canteens from the cool wave. But as they look up they see a cloud of dust rolling up from the plain beyond, and their thirst has passed away—they know that the foe is there.

An aid comes spurring down the bank, waving his hand and splashing into the stream.

"Forward, men! forward!"

Hunter gallops to meet him, with his staff clattering at his horse's heels.

"Break the heads of regiments from the column and push on—push on!"

The field officers dash along the ranks, and the

men spring to their work, as the word of command is echoed from mouth to mouth.

Crossing the stream, their course extended for a mile through a thick wood, but soon they came to the open country, with undulating fields, rolling toward a little valley through which a brooklet ran. And beyond that stream, among the trees and foliage which line its bank and extend in wooded patches southward, the left wing of the enemy are in battle order.

From a clump of bushes directly in front, came a puff of white smoke wreathed with flame; the whir of the hollow ball is heard, and it ploughs the moist ground a few rods from our advance.

Scarcely had the dull report reverberated, when, in quick succession, a dozen jets of fire gleamed out, and the shells came plunging into the ranks. Burnside's brigade was in advance and unsupported, but under the iron hail the line was formed, and the cry "Forward!" was answered with a cheer.. A long grey line spread out upon the hillside, forming rapidly from the outskirts of the little wood. It was the Southern infantry, and soon along their line a deadly fire of musketry was opened.

Meanwhile the heavy firing from the left and further on, announced that the centre and extreme left were engaged. A detachment of regulars was sent to Burnside's relief, and held the enemy in check till a portion of Porter's and Heintzelman's division came up and pressed them back from their position.

The battle was fiercely raging in the centre, where the 69th had led the van and were charging the murderous batteries with the bayonet. We must leave their deeds to be traced by the historic pen, and confine our narrative to the scene in which Harold bore a part. The nearest battery, supported by Carolinians, had been silenced. The Mississippians had wavered before successive charges, and an Alabama regiment, after four times hurling back the serried ranks that dashed against them, had fallen back, outflanked and terribly cut up. On the left was a farm-house, situated on an elevated ridge a little back from the road. Within, while the fiercest battle raged, was its solitary inmate, an aged and bed-ridden lady, whose paralyzed and helpless form was stretched upon the bed where for fourscore years she had slept the calm sleep of a Christian. She had sent her attendants from the dwelling to seek a place of safety, but would not herself consent to be removed, for she heard the whisper of the angel of death, and chose to meet him there in the house of her childhood. For the possession of the hill on which the building stood, the opposing hosts were hotly struggling. The fury of the battle seemed to concentre there, and through the time-worn walls the shot was plunging, splintering the planks and beams, and shivering the stone foundation. Sherman's battery came thundering up the hill upon its last desperate advance. Just as the foaming horses were wheeled upon its summit, the van of Hampton's legion sprang up the opposite side, and the crack of a hundred rifles simultaneously sounded. Down fell the cannoneers beside their guns before those deadly missiles, and the plunging horses were slaughtered in the traces, or, wounded to the death, lashed out their iron hoofs among the maimed and writhing soldiers and into the heaps of dead. The battery was captured, but held only for an instant, when two companies of Rhode Islanders, led on by Harold Hare, charged madly up the hill.

"Save the guns, boys!" he cried, as the gallant fellows bent their heads low, and sprang up the ascent right in the face of the blazing rifles.

"Fire low! stand firm! drive them back once again, my brave Virginians!" shouted a young Southern officer, springing to the foremost rank.

The mutual fire was delivered almost at the rifles' muzzles, and the long sword-bayonets clashed together. Without yielding ground, for a few terrible seconds they thrust and parried with the clanging steel, while on either side the dead were stiffening beneath their feet, and the wounded, with shrieks of agony, were clutching at their limbs. Harold and the young Southron met; their swords clashed together once in the smoke and dust, and but once, when each drew back and lowered his weapon, while all around were striking. Then, amid that terrible discord, their two left hands were pressed together for an instant, and a low "God bless you!" came from the lips of both.

"To the right, Beverly, keep you to the

right!" said Harold, and he himself, straight through the hostile ranks, sprang in an opposite direction.

When Harold's party had first charged up the hill, the young lieutenant with whom he had conversed beside the watch-fire on the previous evening, was at the head of his platoon, and as the two bodies met, he sent the last shot from his revolver full in the faces of the foremost rank. So close were they, that the victim of that shot, struck in the centre of the forehead, tottered forward, and fell into his arms. There was a cry of horror that pierced even above the shrieks of the wounded and the yells of the fierce combatants. One glance at that fair, youthful face sufficed—it was his brother—dead in his arms, dead by a brother's hand. The yellow hair yet curled above the temples, but the rosy bloom upon the cheek was gone; already the ashen hue of death was there. There was a small round hole just where the golden locks waved from the edge of the brow, and from it there slowly welled a single globule of black gore. It left the face undisfigured—pale, but tranquil and undistorted as a sleeping child's—not even a clot of blood was there to mar its beauty. The strong and manly soldier knelt upon the dust, and holding the dead boy with both arms clasped about his waist, bent his head low down upon the lifeless bosom, and gasped with an agony more terrible than that which the death-wound gives.

"Charley! Oh God! Charley! Charley!" was all that came from his white lips, and he sat there like stone, with the corpse in his arms, still murmuring "Charley!" unconscious that blades were flashing and bullets whistling around him. The blood streamed from his wounds, the bayonets were gleaming round, and once a random shot ploughed into his thigh and shivered the bone. He only bent a little lower and his voice was fainter; but still he murmured "Charley! Oh God! Charley," and never unfolded his arms from its embrace. And there, when the battle was over, the Southrons found him, dead—with his dead brother in his arms.

CHAPTER XXII.

At the door-way of the building on the hill, where the aged invalid was yielding her last breath amid the roar of battle, a wounded officer sat among the dying and the dead, while the conflict swept a little away from that quarter of the field. The blood was streaming from the shattered bosom, and feebly he strove to staunch it with his silken scarf. He had dragged himself through gore and dust until he reached that spot, and now, rising again with a convulsive effort, he leaned his red hands against the wall, and entered over the fragments of the door, which had been shivered by a shell. With tottering steps he passed along the hall and up the little stairway, as one who had been familiar with the place. Before the door of the aged lady's chamber he paused a moment and listened; all was still there, although the terrible tumult of the battle was sounding all around. He entered; he advanced to the bed-side; the dying woman was murmuring a prayer. A random shot had torn the shrivelled flesh upon her bosom and the white counterpane was stained with blood. She did not see him—her thoughts were away from earth, she was already seeking communion with the spirits of the blest. The soldier knelt by that strange death-bed and leaned his pale brow upon the pillow.

"Mother!"

How strangely the word sounded amid the shouts of combatants and the din of war. It was like a good angel's voice drowning the discords of hell.

"Mother!"

She heard not the cannon's roar, but that one word, scarce louder than the murmur of a dreaming infant, reached her ear. The palsied head was turned upon the pillow and the light of life returned to her glazing eyes.

"Who speaks?" she gasped, while her thin hands were tremulously clasped together with emotion.

"'Tis I, mother. Philip, your son."

"Philip, my son!" and the nerveless form,

that had scarce moved for years, was raised upon the bed by the last yearning effort of a mother's love.

"Is it you, Philip, is it you, indeed? I can scarce see your form, but surely I have heard the voice of my boy—my long absent boy. Oh! Philip! why have I not heard it oftener to comfort my old age?"

"I am dying, mother. I have been a bad son and a guilty man. But I am dying, mother. Oh! I am punished for my sin! The avenging bullet struck me down at the gate of the home I had deserted—the home I have made desolate to you. Mother, I have crawled here to die."

"To die! O God! your hand is cold—or is it but the chill of death upon my own? Oh! I had thought to have said farewell to earth forever, but yet let me linger but a little while, O Lord! if but to bless my son." She sank exhausted upon the pillow, but yet clasped the gory fingers of the dying man.

"Philip, are you there? Let me hear your voice. I hear strange murmurs afar off; but not the voice of my son. Are you there, Philip, are you there?"

Philip Searle was crouching lower and lower by the bed-side, and his forehead, upon which the dews of death were starting, lay languidly beside the thin, white locks that rested on the pillow.

"Look, mother!" he said, raising his head and glaring into the corner of the room. "Do you see that form in white?—there—she with the pale cheeks and golden hair! I saw her once before to-day, when she lay stretched upon the bed, with a lily in her white fingers. And once again I saw her in that last desperate charge, when the bullet struck my side. And now she is there again, pale, motionless, but smiling. Does she smile in mockery or forgiveness? I could rather bear a frown than that terrible—that frozen smile. O God! she is coming to me, mother, she is coming to me—she will lay her cold hand upon me. No—it is not she! it is Moll—look, mother, it is Moll, all blackened with smoke and seared with living fire. O God! how terrible! But, mother, I did not do that. When I saw the flames afar off, I shuddered, for I knew how it must be. But I did not do it, Moll, by my lost soul, I did not!" He started to his feet with a convulsive effort.

The hot blood spurted from his wound with the exertion and spattered upon the face and breast of his mother—but she felt it not, for she was dead. The last glimmering ray of reason seemed to drive away the phantoms. He turned toward those sharp and withered features, he saw the fallen jaw and lustreless glazed eye. A shudder shook his frame at every point, and with a groan of pain and terror, he fell forward upon the corpse—a corpse himself.

CHAPTER XXIII.

The Federal troops, with successive charges, had now pushed the enemy from their first position, and the torn battalions were still being hurled against the batteries that swept their ranks. The excellent generalship of the Confederate leaders availed itself of the valor and impetuosity of their assailants to lure them, by consecutive advance and backward movement, into the deadly range of their well planted guns. It was then that, far to the right, a heavy column could be seen moving rapidly in the rear of the contending hosts. Was it a part of Hunter's division that had turned the enemy's rear? Such was the thought at first, and with the delusion triumphant cheers rang from the parched throats of the weary Federals. They were soon to be undeceived. The stars and bars flaunted amid those advancing ranks, and the constant yells of the Confederates proclaimed the truth. Johnston was pouring his fresh troops upon the battle-field. The field was lost, but still was struggled for in the face of hope. It was now late in the afternoon, and the soldiers, exhausted with their desperate exertions, fought on, doggedly, but without that fiery spirit which earlier in the day had urged them to the cannon's mouth. There was a lull in the storm of carnage, the brief pause that precedes the last terrific fury of the tempest. The Confederates were concentrating their energies for a decisive effort. It came. From the woods that skirted the left centre of their position, a squadron of horsemen came thundering down upon our columns. Right down upon Carlisle's battery they rode, slashing the cannoneers and capturing the guns. Then followed their rushing ranks of infantry, and full upon our flank swooped down another troop of cavalry, dashing into the road where the baggage-train had been incautiously advanced. Our tired and broken regiments were scattered to the right and left. In vain a few devoted officers spurred among them, and called on them to rally; they broke from the ranks in every quarter of the field, and rushed madly up the hillsides and into the shelter of the trees. The magnificent army that had hailed the rising sun with hopes of victory was soon pouring along the road in inextricable confusion and disorderly retreat. Foot soldier and horseman, field-piece and wagon, caisson and ambulance, teamster and cannoneer, all were mingled together and rushing backward from the field they had half won, with their backs to the pursuing foe. That rout has been traced, to our shame, in history; the pen of the novelist shuns the disgraceful theme.

Harold, although faint with loss of blood, which oozed from a flesh-wound in his shoulder, was among the gallant few who strove to stem the ebbing current; struck at last by a spent ball in the temple, he fell senseless to the ground. He would have been trampled upon and crushed by the retreating column, had not a friendly hand dragged him from the road to a little mound over which spread the branches of an oak. Here he was found an hour afterward by a body of Confederate troops and lifted into an ambulance with others wounded and bleeding like himself.

While the vehicle, with its melancholy freight,

was being slowly trailed over the scene of the late battle, Harold partially recovered his benumbed senses. He lay there as in a dream, striving to recall himself to consciousness of his position. He felt the dull throbbing pain upon his brow and the stinging sensation in his shoulder, and knew that he was wounded, but whether dangerously or not he could not judge. He could feel the trickling of blood from the bosom of a wounded comrade at his side, and could hear the groans of another whose thigh was shattered by the fragment of a shell; but the situation brought no feeling of repugnance, for he was yet half stunned and lay as in a lethargy, wishing only to drain one draught of water and then to sleep. The monotonous rumbling of the ambulance wheels sounded distinctly upon his ear, and he could listen, with a kind of objectless curiosity, to the casual conversation of the driver, as he exchanged words here and there with others, who were returning upon the same dismal errand from the scene of carnage. The shadows of night spread around him, covering the field of battle like a pall flung in charity by nature over the corpses of the slain. Then his bewildered fancies darkened with the surrounding gloom, and he thought that he was coffined and in a hearse, being dragged to the graveyard to be buried. He put forth his hand to push the coffin lid, but it fell again with weakness, and when his fingers came in contact with the splintered bone that protruded from his neighbor's thigh, and he felt the warm gushing of the blood that welled with each throb of the hastily bound artery, he puzzled his dreamy thoughts to know what it might mean. At last all became a blank upon his brain, and he relapsed once more into unconsciousness.

And so, from dreamy wakefulness to total oblivion he passed to and fro, without an interval to part the real from the unreal. He was conscious of being lifted into the arms of men, and being borne along carefully by strong arms. Whither? It seemed to his dull senses that they were bearing him into a sepulchre, but he was not terrified, but careless and resigned; or if he thought of it at all, it was to rejoice that when laid there, he should be undisturbed. Presently a vague fancy passed athwart his mind, that perhaps the crawling worms would annoy him, and he felt uneasy, but yet not afraid. Afterward, there was a sensation of quiet and relief, and his brain, for a space, was in repose. Then a bright form bent over him, and he thought it was an angel. He could feel a soft hand brushing the dampness from his brow, and fingers, whose light touch soothed him, parting his clotted hair. The features grew more distinct, and it pleased him to look upon them, although he strove in vain to fix them in his memory, until a tear-drop fell upon his cheek, and recalled his wandering senses; then he knew that Oriana was bending over him and weeping.

He was in the cottage where Beverly had last parted from his sister; not in the same room, for they feared to place him there, where Miranda was lying in a shroud, with a coffin by her bed-side, lest the sad spectacle should disturb him when he woke. But he lay upon a comfortable bed in another room, and Beverly and Oriana stood beside, while the surgeon dressed his wounds.

CHAPTER XXIV.

No need to say that Harold was well cared for by his two friendly foes. Beverly had given his personal parole for his safe keeping, and he was therefore free from all surveillance or annoyance on that score. His wounds were not serious, although the contusion on the temple, which, however, had left the skull uninjured, occasioned some uneasiness at first. But the third day he was able to leave his bed, and with his arm in a sling, sat comfortably in an easy-chair, and conversed freely with his two excellent nurses.

"Did Beverly tell you of Arthur's imprisonment?" he asked of Oriana, breaking a pause in the general conversation.

"Yes," she answered, looking down, with a scarcely perceptible blush upon her cheek. "Poor Arthur! Yours is a cruel government, Harold, that would make traitors of such men.

His noble heart would not harbor a dangerous thought, much less a traitorous design."

"I think with you," said Harold. "There is some strange mistake, which we must fathom. I received his letter only the day preceding the battle. Had there been no immediate prospect of an engagement, I would have asked a furlough, and have answered it in person. I have small reason to regret my own imprisonment," he added, "my jailers are so kind; yet I do regret it for his sake."

"You know that we are powerless to help him," said Beverly, "or even to shorten your captivity, since your government will not exchange with us. However, you must write, both to Arthur and to Mr. Lincoln, and I will use my best interest with the general to have your letters sent on with a flag."

"I know that you will do all in your power, and I trust that my representations may avail with the government, for I judge from Arthur's letter that he is not well, although he makes no complaint. He is but delicate at the best, and what with the effects of his late injuries, I fear that the restraint of a prison may go ill with him."

"How unnatural is this strife that makes us sorrow for our foes no less than for our friends?" said Oriana. "I seem to be living in a strange clime, and in an age that has passed away. And how long can friendship endure this fiery ordeal? How many scenes of carnage like this last terrible one can afflict the land, without wiping away all trace of brotherhood, and leaving in the void the seed of deadly hate?"

"If this repulse," said Beverly, "which your arms have suffered so early in the contest, will awaken the North to a sense of the utter futility of their design of subjugation, the blood that flowed at Manassas will not have been shed in vain."

"No, not in vain," replied Harold, "but its fruits will be other than you anticipate. The North will be awakened, but only to gird up its loins and put forth its giant strength. The shame of that one defeat will be worth to us hereafter a hundred victories. The North has has been smitten in its sleep; it will arouse from its lethargy like a lion awakening under the smart of the hunter's spear. Beverly, base no vain hopes upon the triumph of the hour; it seals your doom, for it serves but to throw into the scale against you the aroused energies that till now have been withheld."

"You count upon your resources, Harold, like a purse-proud millionaire, who boasts his bursting coffers. We depend rather upon our determined hearts and resolute right hands. Upon our power to endure, greater than yours to inflict, reverse. Upon our united people, and the spirit that animates them, which can never be subdued. The naked Britons could defend their native soil against Cæsar's legions, the veterans of a hundred fights. Shall we do less, who have already tasted the fruits of liberty so dearly earned? Harold, your people have assumed an impossible task, and you may as well go cast your treasures into the sea as squander them in arms to smite your kith and kin. We are Americans, like yourselves; and when you confess that *you* can be conquered by invading armies, then dream of conquering us."

"And we will startle you from your dream with the crack of our Southern rifles," added Oriana, somewhat maliciously, while Harold smiled at her enthusiasm.

"There is a great deal of romance in both your natures," he replied. "But it is not so good as powder for a fighting medium. The spirit you boast of will not support you long without the aid of good round dollars."

"Thank heaven we have less faith in their efficacy than you Northern gold-worshippers," observed Oriana, with playful sarcasm. "While our soldiers have good round corn-cakes, they will ask for no richer metals than lead and steel. Have you never heard of the regiment of Mississippians, who, having received their pay in government certificates, to a man tore up the documents as they took up the line of march, saying 'we do not fight for money?'"

Harold smiled, thinking perhaps that nothing better could have been done with the currency in question.

"I think," said Beverly, "you are far out of the way in your estimate of our resources. The South is strictly an agricultural country, and as such, best able to support itself under the exhaustion consequent upon a lengthened warfare, especially as it will remain in the attitude of resistance to invasion. From the bosom of its prolific soil it can draw its natural nourishment and retain its vigor throughout any period of isolation, while you are draining your resources for the means of providing an active aggressive warfare. The rallying of our white population to the battle field will not interrupt the course of agricultural pursuit, while every enlistment in the North will take one man away from the tillage of the land or from some industrial avocation."

"Not so," replied Harold. "Our armies for the most part will be recruited from the surplus population, and abundant hands will remain behind for the purposes of industry."

"At first, perhaps. But not after a few more such fields as were fought on Sunday last. To carry out even a show of your project of subjugation, you must keep a million of men in the field from year to year. Your manufacturing interests will be paralyzed, your best customers shut out. You will be spending enormously and producing little beyond the necessities of consumption. We, on the contrary, will be producing as usual, and spending little more than before."

"Can your armies be fed, clothed, and equipped without expense?"

"No. But all our means will be applied to military uses, and our operations will be necessarily much less expensive than yours. In other matters, we will forget our habits of extravagance. We will become, by the law of necessity, economists in place of spendthrifts. We will gather in rich harvests, but will stint ourselves to the bare necessities of life, that our troops may be fed and clothed. The money that our wealthy planters have been in the habit of spending yearly in Northern cities and watering places, will be circulated at home. Some fifty millions of Southern dollars, heretofore annually wasted in fashionable dissipation, will thus be kept in our own pockets and out of yours. The spendthrift sons of our planters, and their yet more extravagant daughters, will be found studying economy in the rude school of the soldier, and plying the needle to supply the soldiers' wants, in place of drawing upon the paternal estates for frivolous enjoyments. Our spending population will be on the battle-field, and the laborer will remain in the cotton and corn-field. There will be suffering and privation, it is true, but rest assured, Harold, we will bear it all without a murmur, as our fathers did in the days of '76. And we will trust to the good old soil we are defending to give us our daily bread."

"Or if it should not," said Oriana, "we can at least claim from it, each one, a grave, over which the foot of the invader may trample, but not over our living bodies."

"I have no power to convince you of your error," answered Harold. "Let us speak of it no more, since it is destined that the sword must decide between us. Beverly, you promised that I should go visit my wounded comrades, who have not yet been removed. Shall we go now? I think it would do me good to breathe the air."

They prepared for the charitable errand, and Oriana went with them, with a little basket of delicacies for the suffering prisoners.

CHAPTER XXV.

It was a fair morning in August, the twentieth day after the eventful 21st of July. Beverly was busy with his military duties, and Harold, who had already fully recovered from his wounds, was enjoying, in company with Oriana, a pleasant canter over the neighboring country. They came to where the rolling meadow subsided into a level plain of considerable extent on either side of the road. At its verge a thick forest formed a dark background, beyond which the peering summits of green hills showed that the landscape was rugged and uneven. Oriana slackened her pace, and pointed out over the broad expanse of level country.

"You see this plain that stretches to our right and left?"

"Of course I do," replied Harold.

"Yes; but I want you to mark it well," she continued, with a significant glance; "and also that stretch of woodland yonder, beyond which, you see, the country rises again."

"Yes, a wild country, I should judge, like that to the left, where we fought your batteries a month ago."

"It is, indeed, a wild country as you say. There are ravines there, and deep glens, fringed with almost impenetrable shrubbery, and deep down in these recesses flows many a winding water-course, lined and overarched with twisted foliage. Are you skillful at threading a woodland labyrinth?"

"Yes; my surveying expeditions have schooled me pretty well. Why do you ask? Do you want me to guide you through the wilderness, in search of a hermit's cave."

"Perhaps; women have all manner of caprices, you know. But I want you to pay attention to those landmarks. Over yonder, there are some nooks that would do well to hide a runaway. I have explored some of them myself, for I passed some months here formerly, before the war. Poor Miranda's family resided once in the little cottage where we are stopping now. That is why I came from Richmond to spend a few days and be with Beverly. I little thought that my coming would bring me to Miranda's death-bed. Look there, now: you have a better view of where the forest ascends into the hilly ground."

"Why are you so topographical to-day? One would think you were tempting me to run away," said Harold, smiling, as he followed her pointing finger with his eyes.

"No; I know you would not do that, because Beverly, you know, has pledged himself for your safe-keeping.

"Very true; and I am therefore a closer prisoner than if I were loaded down with chains. When do you return to Richmond?"

"I shall return on the day after to-morrow. Beverly has been charged with an important service, and will be absent for several weeks. But he can procure your parole, if you wish, and you can come to the old manor-house again."

"I think I shall not accept parole," replied Harold, thoughtfully. "I must escape, if possible, for Arthur's sake. Beverly, of course, will release himself from all obligations about me, before he goes?"

"Yes, to-morrow; but you will be strictly guarded, unless you give parole. See here, I have a little present for you; it is not very pretty, but it is useful."

She handed him a small pocket-compass, set in a brass case.

"You can have this too," she added, drawing a small but strong and sharp poignard from her bosom. "But you must promise me never to use it except to save your life?"

"I will promise that cheerfully," said Harold, as he received the precious gifts.

"To-morrow we will ride out again. We will have the same horses that bear us so bravely now. Do you note how strong and well-bred is the noble animal you ride?"

"Yes," said Harold, patting the glorious arch of his steed's neck. "He's a fine fellow, and fleet, I warrant."

"Fleet as the winds. There are few in this neighborhood that can match him. Let us go home now. You need not tell Beverly that I have given you presents. And be ready to ride to-morrow at four o'clock precisely."

He understood her thoroughly, and they cantered homeward, conversing upon indifferent subjects and reverting no further to their previous somewhat enigmatical theme.

On the following afternoon, at four o'clock precisely, the horses were at the door, and five minutes afterward a mounted officer, followed by two troopers, galloped up the lane and drew rein at the gateway.

Harold was arranging the girths of Oriana's saddle, and she herself was standing in her riding-habit beside the porch. The officer, dismounting, approached her and raised his cap in respectful salute. He was young and well-looking, evidently one accustomed to polite society.

"Good afternoon, Captain Haralson," said Oriana, with her most gracious smile. "I am very glad to see you, although, as you bring your military escort, I presume you come to see Beverly upon business, and not for the friendly visit you promised me. But Beverly is not here."

"I left him at the camp on duty, Miss Weems," replied the captain. "It is my misfortune that my own duties have been too strict of late to permit me the pleasure of my contemplated visit."

"I must bide my time, captain. Let me introduce my friend, Captain Hare, our prisoner, Mr. Haralson; but I know you will help me to make him forget it, when I tell you that he was my brother's schoolmate and is our old and valued friend."

The young officer took Harold frankly by the hand, but he looked grave and somewhat disconcerted as he answered:

"Captain Hare, as a soldier, will forgive me that my duty compels me to play a most ungracious part upon our first acquaintance. I have orders to return with him to headquarters, where I trust his acceptance of parole will enable me to avail myself of your introduction to show him what courtesy our camp life admits, in atonement for the execution of my present unpleasant devoir."

"I shall esteem your acquaintance the more highly," answered Harold, "that you know so well to blend your soldiership with kindness. I am entirely at your disposition, sir, having only to apologize to Miss Weems for the deprivation of her contemplated ride."

"Oh, no, we must not lose our ride," said Oriana. "It is perhaps the last we shall enjoy together, and such a lovely afternoon. I am sure that Captain Haralson is too gallant to interrupt our excursion."

She turned to him with an arch smile, but he looked serious as he replied:

"Alas! Miss Weems, our gallantry receives some rude rebuffs in the harsh school of the soldier. It grieves me to mar your harmless recreation, but even that mortification I must endure when it comes in the strict line of my duty."

"But your duty does not forbid you to take a canter with us this charming afternoon. Now put away that military sternness, which does not become you at all, and help me to mount my pretty Nelly, who is getting impatient to be off. And so am I. Come, you will get into camp in due season, for we will go only as far as the Run, and canter all the way."

She took his arm, and he assisted her to the saddle, won into acquiescence by her graceful obstinacy, and, in fact, seeing but little harm in the slight departure from the strict performance of his errand. They mounted and rode out together, Oriana leading the way, and choosing the path they had followed on the preceding day.

"Keep us within sight, but you need not press too closely upon us," said Captain Haralson to the two troopers as he passed. The men followed the cavalcade, riding far enough in the background to avoid the appearance of being an armed escort.

The afternoon was truly delightful, and the polite young Southron, too much an admirer of beauty to fail of appreciating the opportunity of caracolling by the side of so charming a horsewoman as Oriana, soon lost all sense of uneasiness in the pleasure he derived from her company and conversation. Harold at first was taciturn, but his reserve soon gave way before the inevitable exhilaration produced by the combined influences of bracing air, exercise, good company, and lovely scenery.

"Do you think we will let you Northerners drive us from such scenery as that?" said Oriana, good naturedly, pointing with her whip to where the tufted hills rolled into one another like the waves of a swelling sea, their crests tipped with the slant rays of the descending sun, and their graceful slopes alternating among purple shadows and gleams of floating light.

"It is indeed so beautiful," answered Harold, "that I should deem you might be content to live there as of old, without inviting the terrible companionship of Mars."

"We do not invite it," said the young captain. "Leave us in peaceful possession of our own, and no war cries shall echo among those hills. If Mars has driven his chariot into our homes, he comes at your bidding, an unwelcome intruder, to be scourged back again."

"At our bidding! No. The first gun that was fired at Sumter summoned him, and if he should leave his foot-prints deep in your soil, you have well earned the penalty."

"It will cost you, to inflict it, many such another day's work as that at Manassas a month ago."

The taunt was spoken hastily, and the young Southron colored as if ashamed of his discourtesy, and added:

"Forgive me my ungracious speech. It was my first field, sir, and I am wont to speak of it too boastingly. I shall become more modest, I hope, when I shall have a better right to be a boaster."

"Oh," replied Harold, "I admit the shame of our discomfiture, and take it as a good lesson to our negligence and want of purpose. But all that has passed away. One good whipping has awakened us to an understanding of the work we have in hand. Henceforth we will apply ourselves to the task in earnest."

"You think, then, that your government will prosecute the war more vigorously than before?"

"Undoubtedly. You have heard but the prelude of a gale that shall sweep every vestige of treason from the land."

"Let it blow on," said the Southron, proudly. "There will be counter-blasts to meet it. You cannot raise a tempest that will make us bow our heads."

"Do you not think," interrupted Oriana, "that a large proportion of your Northern population are ready at least to listen to terms of separation?"

"No," replied Harold, firmly. "Or if there be

any who entertain such thoughts, we will make them outcasts among us, and the finger of scorn will be pointed at them as recreant to their holiest duty."

"That is hardly fair," said Oriana. "Why should you scorn or maltreat those who honestly believe that the doctrine in support of which so many are ready to stake their lives and their fortunes, may be worthy of consideration? Do you believe us all mad and wicked people in the South—people without hearts, and without brains, incapable of forming an opinion that is worth an argument? If there are some among you who think we are acting for the best, and Heaven knows we are acting with sincerity, you should give them at least a hearing, for the sake of liberty of conscience. Remember, there are millions of us united in sentiment in the South, and millions, perhaps, abroad who think with us. How can you decide by your mere impulses where the right lies?"

"We decide by the promptings of our loyal hearts, and by our reason, which tells us that secession is treason, and that treason must be crushed."

"Heart and brain have been mistaken ere now," returned Oriana. "But if you are a type of your countrymen, I see that hard blows alone will teach you that God has given us the right to think for ourselves."

"Do you believe, then," asked Haralson, "that there can be no peace between us until one side or the other shall be exhausted and subdued?"

"Not so," replied Harold. "I think that when we have retrieved the disgrace of Bull Run and given you in addition, some wholesome chastisement, your better judgment will return to you, and you will accept forgiveness at our hands and return to your allegiance."

"You are mistaken," said the Southron. "Even were we ready to accept your terms, you would not be ready to grant them. Should the North succeed in striking some heavy blow at the South, I will tell you what will happen; your abolitionists will seize the occasion of the peoples' exultation to push their doctrine to a consummation. Whenever you shall hear the tocsin of victory sounding in the North, then listen for the echoing cry of emancipation—for you will hear it. You will see it in every column of your daily prints; you will hear your statesmen urging it in your legislative halls, and your cabinet ministers making it their theme. And, most dangerous of all, you will hear your generals and colonels, demagogues at heart, and soldiers only of occasion, preaching it to their battalions, and making converts of their subordinates by the mere influences of their rank and calling. And when your military chieftains harangue their soldiers upon political themes, think not of our treason, as you call it, but look well to the political freedom that is still your own. With five hundred thousand armed puppets, moving at the will of a clique of ambitious epauletted politicians and experimentalists, you may live to witness, whether we be subdued or not, a *coup d'état* for which there is a precedent not far back in the annals of republics."

"Have you already learned to contemplate the danger that you are incurring? Do you at last fear the monster that you have nursed and strengthened in your midst? Well, if your slaves should rise against you, surely you cannot blame us for the evil of your own creation."

"It is the hope of your abolitionists, not our fear, that I am rehearsing. Should your armies obtain a foothold on our soil, we know that you will put knives and guns into the hands of our slaves, and incite them to emulate the deeds of their race in San Domingo. You will parcel out our lands and wealth to your victorious soldiery, not so much as a reward for their past services, but to seal the bond between them and the government that will seek to rule by their bayonets. You see, we know the peril and are prepared to meet it. Should you conquer us, at the same time you would conquer the liberties of the Northern citizen. You will be at the mercy of the successful general whose triumph may make him the idol of the armed millions that alone can accomplish our subjugation. In the South, butchery and rapine by hordes of desperate negroes—in the North anarchy and political intrigue, to be merged into dictatorship and the absolutism of military power. Such would be the results of your triumph and our defeat."

"Those are the visions of a heated brain," said Harold. "I must confess that your fighting is better than your logic. There is no danger to our country that the loyalty of its people cannot overcome—as it will your rebellion."

CHAPTER XXVI.

They had now approached the edge of the plain which Oriana had pointed out on the preceding day. The sun, which had been tinging the western sky with gorgeous hues, was peering from among masses of purple and golden clouds, within an hour's space of the horizon. Captain Haralson, interested and excited by his disputation, had been riding leisurely along by the side of his prisoner, taking but little note of the route or of the lapse of time.

"Cease your unprofitable argument," cried Oriana, "and let us have a race over this beautiful plain. Look! 'tis as smooth as a race-course, and I will lay you a wager, Captain Haralson, that my Nelly will lead you to yonder clump, by a neck."

She touched her horse lightly with the whip, and turned from the road into the meadows.

"It is late, Miss Weems," said the Southron, "and I must report at headquarters before sundown. Besides, I am badly mounted, and it would be but a sorry victory to distance me. I pray you, let us return."

"Nonsense! Nelly is not breathed. I must have one fair run over this field; and, gentlemen, I challenge you both to outstrip Nelly if you can."

With a merry shout, she struck the fleet mare smartly on the flank, and the spirited animal, more at the sound of her voice than aroused by the whip-lash, stretched forward her neck and sprang over the tufted level. Harold waved his hand, as if in invitation, to his companion, and was soon urging his powerful horse in the same direction. Haralson shouted to them to stop, but they only turned their heads and beckoned to him gaily, and plunging the spurs into the strong but heavy-hoofed charger that he rode, he followed them as best he could. He kept close in their rear very well at first, but he soon observed that he was losing distance, and that the two swift steeds in front, that had been held in check a little at the start, were now skimming the smooth meadow at a tremendous pace.

"Halt!" he cried, at the top of his lungs; but

either they heard it not or heeded it not, for they still swept on, bending low forward in the saddle, almost side by side.

A vague suspicion crossed his mind.

"Halt, there!"

Oriana glanced over her shoulder, and could see a sunray gleaming from something that he held in his right hand. He had drawn a pistol from his holster. She slackened her pace a little, and allowing Harold to take the lead, rode on in the line between him and the pursuer. Harold turned in his saddle. She could hear the tones of his voice rushing past her on the wind.

"Come no further with me, lest suspicion attach to yourself. The good horse will bear me beyond pursuit. Remember, it is for Arthur's sake I have consented you should make this sacrifice. God bless you! and farewell!"

A pistol-shot resounded in the air. Oriana knew it was fired but to intimidate—the distance was too great to give the leaden messenger a deadlier errand. Yet she drew rein, and waited, breathless with excitement and swift motion, till Haralson came up. He turned one reproachful glance upon her as he passed, and spurred on in pursuit. Harold turned once again, to assure himself that she was unhurt, then waved his hand, and urging his swift steed to the utmost, sped on toward the forest which was now close at hand. The two troopers soon came galloping up to where Oriana still sat motionless upon her saddle, watching the race with strained eyes and heaving bosom.

"Your prisoner has escaped," she said; "spur on in pursuit."

She knew that it was of no avail, for Harold had already disappeared among the mazes of the wood, and the sun was just dipping below the horizon. Darkness would soon shroud the fugitive in its friendly mantle. She turned Nelly's head homeward, and cantered silently away in the gathering twilight.

CHAPTER XXVII.

When Captain Haralson and the two troopers reached the verge of the forest, they could trace for a short distance the hoof-prints of Harold's horse, and followed them eagerly among the labyrinthine paths which the fugitive had made through the tangled shrubbery and among the briery thickets. But soon the gloom of night closed in upon them in the depth of the silent wood, and they were left without a sign by which to direct the pursuit. It was near midnight when they reached the further edge of the forest, and there, throwing fantastic gleams of red light among the shadows of the tall trees, they caught sight of what seemed to be the glimmer of a watchfire. Soon after, the growl of a hound was heard, followed by a deep-mouthed bay, and approaching cautiously, they were hailed by the watchful sentinel. It was a Confederate picket, posted on the outskirt of the forest, and Haralson, making himself known, rode up to where the party, awakened by their approach, had roused themselves from their blankets, and were standing with ready rifles beside the blazing fagots.

Haralson made known his errand to the officer in command, and the sentries were questioned, but all declared that nothing had disturbed their watch; if the fugitive had passed their line, he had succeeded in eluding their vigilance.

"I must send one of my men back to camp to report the escape," said Haralson, "and will ask you to spare me a couple of your fellows to help me hunt the Yankee down. Confound him, I deserve to lose my epaulettes for my folly, but I'll follow him to the Potomac, rather than return to headquarters without him."

"Who was it?" asked the officer; "was he of rank?"

"A captain, Captain Hare, well named for his fleetness; but he was mounted superbly, and I suspect the whole thing was cut and dried."

"Hare?" cried a hoarse voice; and the speaker, a tall, lank man, who had been stretched by the fire, with the head of a large, gaunt bloodhound in his lap, rose suddenly and stepped forward.

"Harold Hare, by G—d!" he exclaimed; "I know the fellow. Captain, I'm with you on this hunt, and Bully there, too, who is worth the pair of us. Hey, Bully?"

The dog stretched himself lazily, and lifted his heavy lip with a grin above the formidable fangs that glistened in the gleam of the watchfire.

"You may go," said his officer, " but I can't spare another. You three, with the dog, will be enough. Rawbon's as good a man as you can get, captain. Set a thief to catch a thief, and a Yankee to outwit a Yankee. You'd better start at once, unless you need rest or refreshment."

"Nothing," replied Haralson. "Let your man put something into his haversack. Good night, lieutenant. Come along, boys, and keep your eyes peeled, for these Yankees are slippery eels, you know."

Seth Rawbon had already bridled his horse that was grazing hard by, and the party, with the hound close at his master's side, rode forth upon their search.

CHAPTER XXVIII.

Harold had perceived the watchfire an hour earlier than his pursuers, having obtained thus much the advantage of them by the fleetness of his steed. He moved well off to the right, riding slowly and cautiously, until another faint glimmer in that direction gave him to understand that he was about equi-distant between two pickets of the enemy. He dismounted at the edge of the forest, and securing his steed to the branch of a tree, crept forward a few paces beyond the shelter of the wood, and looked about earnestly in the darkness. Nothing could be seen but the long, straggling line of the forest losing itself in the gloom, and the black outlines of the hills before him; but his quick ear detected the sound of coming hoof and the ringing of steel scabbards. A patrol was approaching, and fearful that his horse, conscious of the neighborhood of his kind, might betray his presence with a sign of recognition, he hurried back, and standing beside the animal, caressed his glossy neck and won his attention with the low murmurs of his voice. The good steed remained silent, only pricking up his ears and peering through the branches as the patrol went clattering by. Harold waited till the trampling of hoofs died away in the distance, and judging, from their riding on without a challenge or a pause, that there was no sentry within hail, he mounted and rode boldly out into the open country. The stars were mostly obscured by heavy clouds, but here and there was a patch of clear blue sky, and his eye, practised with many a surveying night-tramp, discovered at last a twinkling guide by which to shape his path in a northerly direction. It was a wild, rough country over which he passed. With slow and careful steps, his sagacious steed moved on, obedient to the rein, at one time topping the crest of a rugged hill, and then winding at a snail's pace down the steep declivity, or following the tortuous course of the streamlet through deep ravines, whose jagged and bush-clad sides frowned down upon them on either side, deepening the gloom of night.

So all through the long hours of darkness, Harold toiled on his lonely way, startled at times by the shriek of the night bird, and listening intently to catch the sign of danger. At last the dawn, welcome although it enhanced the chances of detection, blushed faintly through the clouded eastern sky, and Harold, through the mists of morning, could see a fair and rolling landscape stretched before him. The sky was overcast, and presently the heavy drops began to fall. Consulting the little friendly compass which Oriana had given him, he pushed on briskly, turning always to the right or left, as the smoke, circling from some early housewife's kitchen, betrayed the dangerous neighborhood of a human habitation.

Crossing a rivulet, he dismounted, and filled a small leathern bottle that he carried with him, his good steed and himself meanwhile satisfying their thirst from the cool wave. His appetite, freshened by exercise, caused him to remember a package which Oriana's forethought had provided for him on the preceding afternoon. He drew it from his pocket, and while his steed clipped the tender herbage from the streamlet's bank, he made an excellent breakfast of the corn bread and bacon, and other substantial edibles, which his kind friend had bountifully supplied. Man and horse thus refreshed, he remounted, and rode forward at a gallant pace, the strong animal he bestrode seeming as yet to show no signs of fatigue.

The rain was now falling in torrents, a propitious circumstance, since it lessened the probabilities of his encountering the neighboring inhabitants, most of whom must have sought shelter from the pelting storm. He occasionally came up with a trudging negro, sometimes a group of three or four, who answered timidly whenever he accosted them, and glanced at him askance, but yet gave the information he requested. Once, indeed, he could discern a troop of cavalry plashing along at some distance through the muddy road, but he screened himself in a cornfield, and was unobserved. His watch had been injured in the battle, and he had no means, except conjecture, of judging of the hour; but by the flagging pace of his horse, and his own fatigue, he knew that he must have been many hours in the saddle. Surely the Potomac must be at hand! Yet there was no sign of it, and over interminable hill and dale, through corn-fields, and over patches of woodland and meadow, the weary steed was urged on, slipping and sliding in the saturated soil. What was that sound which caused his horse to prick up his ears and quicken his pace with the instinct of danger? He heard it himself distinctly. It was the baying of a bloodhound.

"They are on my track!" muttered Harold; "and unless the river is at hand, I am lost. Forward, sir! forward, good fellow!" he shouted cheerily to his horse, and the noble animal, snorting and tossing his silken mane, answered with an effort, and broke into a gallop.

Down one hill into a little valley they pushed on, and up the ascent of another. They reached the crest, and then, thank Heaven! there was the broad river, winding through the valley. Dull and leaden hued as it looked, reflecting the clouded sky, he had never hailed it so joyfully when sparkling with sunbeams as he did at the close of that weary day. Yet the danger was not past; up and down the stream he gazed, and far to the right he could distinguish a group of tents peering from among the foliage of a grove, and marking the site of a Confederate battery. But just in front of him was a cheering sight; an armed schooner swung lazily at anchor in the channel, and the wet bunting that drooped listlessly over her stern, revealed the stars and stripes.

The full tones of the bloodhound's voice aroused him to the necessity of action; he turned in the saddle and glanced over the route he had come. On the crest of the hill beyond that on which he stood, the forms of three horsemen were outlined against the greyish sky. They distinguished him at the same moment, for he could hear their shouts of exultation, borne to him on the humid air.

It was yet a full mile to the river bank, and his horse was almost broken down with fatigue. Dashing his armed heels against the throbbing flanks of the jaded animal, he rushed down the hill in a straight line for the water. The sun was already below the horizon, and darkness was coming on apace. As he pushed on, the shouts of his pursuers rang louder upon his ear at every rod; it was evident that they were fresh mounted, while his own steed was laboring, with a last effort, over the rugged ground, stumbling among stones, and groaning at intervals with the severity of exertion. He could hear the trampling behind him, he could catch the words of triumph that seemed to be shouted almost in his very ear. A bullet whizzed by him, and then another, and with each report there came a derisive cheer. But it was now quite dark, and that, with the rapid motion, rendered him comparatively fearless of being struck. He spurred on, straining his eyes to see what was before him, for it seemed that the ground in front became suddenly and curiously lost in the mist and gloom. Just then, simultaneously with the report of a pistol, he felt his good steed quiver beneath him; a bullet had reached his flank, and the poor animal fell upon his knees and rolled over in the agony of death.

It was well that he had fallen; Harold, thrown forward a few feet, touched the earth upon the edge of the rocky bank that descended precipitously a hundred feet or more to the river—a few steps further, and horse and rider would have plunged over the verge of the bluff.

Harold, though bruised by his fall, was not considerably hurt; without hesitation, he commenced the hazardous descent, difficult by day, but perilous and uncertain in the darkness. Clinging to each projecting rock and feeling cautiously for a foothold among the slippery ledges, he had accomplished half the distance and could already hear the light plashing of the wave upon the boulders below. He heard a voice above, shouting: " Look out for the bluff there, we must be near it !"

The warning came too late. There was a cry of terror—the blended voice of man and horse, startling the night and causing Harold to crouch with instinctive horror close to the dripping rock. There was a rush of wind and the bounding by of a dark whirling body, which rolled over and over, tearing over the sharp angles of the cliff, and scattering the loose fragments of stone over him as he clung motionless to his support. Then there was a dull thump below, and a little afterward a terrible moan, and then all was still.

Harold continued his descent and reached the base of the bluff in safety. Through the darkness he could see a dark mass lying like a shadow among the pointed stones, with the waves of the river rippling about it. He approached it. There lay the steed gasping in the last agony, and the rider beneath him, crushed, mangled and dead. He stooped down by the side of the corpse; it was bent double beneath the quivering body of the dying horse, in such a manner as must have snapped the spine in twain. Harold lifted the head, but let it fall again with a shudder, for his fingers had slipped into the crevice of the cleft skull and were all smeared with the oozing brain. Yet, despite the obscurity and the disfigurement, despite the bursting eyeballs and the clenched jaws through which the blood was trickling, he recognized the features of Seth Rawbon.

No time for contemplation or for revery. There was a scrambling overhead, with now and then a snarl and an angry growl. And further up, he heard the sound of voices, labored and suppressed, as of men who were speaking while toiling at some unwonted exercise. Harold threw off his coat and boots, and waded out into the river. The dark hull of the schooner could be seen looming above the gloomy surface of the water, and he dashed toward it through the deepening wave. There was a splash behind him and soon he could hear the puffing and short breathing of a swimming dog. He was then up to his arm-pits in the water, and a few yards further would bring him off his footing. He determined to wait the onset there, while he could yet stand firm upon the shelving bottom. He had not long to wait. The bloodhound made directly for him; he could see his eyes snapping and glaring like red coals above the black water. Harold braced himself as well as he could upon the yielding sand, and held his poignard, Oriana's welcome gift, with a steady grasp. The dog came so close that his fetid breath played upon Harold's cheek; then he aimed a swift blow at his neck, but the brute dodged it like a fish. Harold lost his balance and fell forward into the water, but in falling, he launched out his left hand and caught the tough loose skin above the animal's shoulder. He held it with the grasp of a drowning man, and over and over they rolled in the water, like two sea monsters at their sport. With all his strength, Harold drew the fierce brute toward him, circling his neck tightly with his left arm, and pressed the sharp blade against his throat. The hot blood gushed out over his hand, but he drove the weapon deeper, slitting the sinewy flesh to the right and left, till the dog ceased to struggle. Then Harold flung the huge carcass from him, and struck out, breathless as he was, for the schooner. It was time, for already his pursuers were upon the bank, aiming their pistol shots at the black spot which they could just distinguish cleaving through the water. But a few vigorous strokes carried him beyond their vision and they ceased firing. Soon he heard the sound of muffled oars and a dark shape seemed to rise from the water in front of him. The watch on board the schooner, alarmed by the firing, had sent a boat's crew to reconnoitre. Harold divined that it was so, and hailing the approaching boat, was taken in, and ten minutes afterward, stood, exhausted but safe, upon the schooner's deck.

CHAPTER XXIX.

With the earliest opportunity, Harold proceeded to Washington, and sought an interview with the President, in relation to Arthur's case. Mr. Lincoln received him kindly, but could give no information respecting the arrest or alleged criminality of his friend. "There were so many and pressing affairs of state that he could find no room for individual cases in his memory." However, he referred him to the Secretary of War, with a request that the latter would look into the matter. By dint of persistent inquiries at various sources, Harold finally ascertained that the prisoner had a few days previously been released, upon the assurance of the surgeon at the fort, that his failing health required his immediate removal. Inquiry had been made into the circumstances leading to his arrest; made too late, however, to benefit the victim of a State mistake, whose delicate health had already been too severely tried by the discomforts attendant upon his situation. However, enough had been ascertained to leave but little doubt as to his innocence; and Arthur, with the ghastly signs of a rapid consumption upon his wan cheek, was dismissed from the portals of a prison, which had already prepared him for the tomb.

Harold hastened to Vermont, whither he knew the invalid had been conveyed. It was toward the close of the first autumn day that he entered the little village, upon whose outskirts was situated the farm of his dying friend. The air was mild and balmy, but the voices of nature seemed to him more hushed than usual, as if in mournful unison with his own sad reveries. He had passed on foot from the village to the farm-house, and when he opened the little white wicket, and walked along the gravelled avenue that led to the flower-clad porch, the willows on either side seemed to droop lower than willows are used to droop, and the soft September air sighed through the swinging boughs, like the prelude of a dirge.

Arthur was reclining upon an easy-chair upon the little porch, and beside him sat a venerable lady, reading from the worn silver-clasped Bible, which rested on her lap. The lady rose when he approached; and Arthur, whose gaze had been wandering among the autumn clouds, that wreathed the points of the far-off mountains, turned his head languidly, when the footsteps broke his dream.

He did not rise. Alas! he was too weak to do so without the support of his aged mother's arm, which had so often cradled him in infancy and had now become the staff of his broken manhood. But a beautiful and happy smile illumined his pale lips, and spread all over the thin and wasted features, like sunlight gleaming on the grey surface of a church-yard stone. He lifted his attenuated hand, and when Harold clasped it, the fingers were so cold and deathlike that their pressure seemed to close about his heart, compressing it, and chilling the life current in his veins.

"I knew that you would come, Harold. Although I read that you were missing at the close of that dreadful battle, something told me that we should meet again. Whether it was a sick man's fancy, or the foresight of a parting soul, it is realized, for you are here. And you come not too soon, Harold," he added, with a pressure of the feeble hand, "for I am going fast—fast from the discords of earth—fast to the calm and harmony beyond!"

"Oh, Arthur, how changed you are!" said Harold, who could not keep from fastening his gaze on the white, sunken cheek and hollow eyes of his dying comrade. "But you will get better now, will you not—now that you are home again, and we can nurse you?"

Arthur shook his head with a mournful smile, and the fit of painful coughing which overtook him answered his friend's vain hope.

"No, Harold, no. All of earth is past to me, even hope. And I am ready, cheerful even, to go, except for the sake of some loved ones that will sorrow for me."

He took his mother's hand as he spoke, and looked at her with touching tenderness, while the poor dame brushed away her tears.

"I have but a brief while to stay behind," she said, "and my sorrow will be less, to know that you have ever been a good son to me. Oh, Mr. Hare, he might have lived to comfort me, and close my old eyes in death, if they had not been so cruel with him, and locked him within prison walls. He, who never dreamed of wrong, and never injured willingly a worm in his path."

"Nay, mother, they were not unkind to me in the fort, and did what they could to make me comfortable. But, Harold, it is wrong. I have thought of it in the long, weary nights in prison, and I have thought of it when I knew that death was beckoning me to come and rest from the thoughts of earth. It is wrong to tamper with the sacred law that shields the citizen. I believe that many a man within those fortress walls is as innocent in the eyes of God as those who sent him there. Yet I accuse none of willful wrong, but only of unconscious error. If the sacrifice of my poor life could shed one ray upon the darkness, I would rejoice to be the victim that I am, of a violated right. But all, statesmen, and chieftains, and humble citizens, are being swept along upon the whirlwinds of passion; all hearts are ablaze with the fiery magnificence of war, and none will take warning till the land shall be desolate, and thousands, stricken in their prime, shall be sleeping—where I shall soon be—beneath the cold sod. I am weary, mother, and chill. Let us go in."

They bore him in and helped him to his bed, where he lay pale and silent, seeming much worse from the fatigue of conversation and the excitement of his meeting with his old college friend. Mrs. Wayne left him in charge of Harold, while she went below to prepare what little nourishment he could take, and to provide refreshment for her guest.

Arthur lay, for a space, with his eyes closed, and apparently in sleep. But he looked up, at last, and stretched out his hand to Harold, who pressed the thin fingers, whiter than the coverlet on which they rested.

"Is mother there?"

"No, Arthur," replied Harold. "Shall I call her?"

"No. I thought to have spoken to you, to-morrow, of something that has been often my theme of thought; but I know not what strange feeling has crept upon me; and perhaps, Harold —for we know not what the morrow may bring— perhaps I had better speak now."

"It hurts you, Arthur; you are too weak. Indeed, you must sleep now, and to-morrow we shall talk."

"No; now, Harold. It will not hurt me, or if it does, it matters little now. Harold, I would fain that no shadow of unkindness should linger between us twain when I am gone."

"Why should there, Arthur? You have been my true friend always, and as such shall I remember you."

"Yet have I wronged you; yet have I caused you much grief and bitterness, and only your own generous nature preserved us from estrangement. Harold, have you heard from *her?*"

"I have seen her, Arthur. During my captivity, she was my jailer; in my sickness, for I was slightly wounded, she was my nurse. I will tell you all about it to-morrow."

"Yes, to-morrow," replied Arthur, breathing heavily. "To-morrow! the word sounds meaningless to me, like something whose significance has left me. Is she well, Harold?"

"Yes."

"And happy?"

"I think so, Arthur. As happy as any of us can be, amid severed ties and dread uncertainties."

"I am glad that she is well. Harold, you will

tell her, for I am sure you will meet again, you will tell her it was my dying wish that you two should be united. Will you promise, Harold?"

"I will tell her all that you wish, Arthur."

"I seem to feel that I shall be happy in my grave, to know that she will be your wife; to know that my guilty love—for I loved her, Harold, and it *was* guilt to love—to know that it left no poison behind, that its shadow has passed away from the path that you must tread."

"Speak not of guilt, my friend. There could live no crime between two such noble hearts. And had I thought you would have accepted the sacrifice, I could almost have been happy to have given her to you, so much was her happiness the aim of my own love."

"Yes, for you have a glorious heart, Harold; and I thank Heaven that she cannot fail to love you. And you do not think, do you, Harold, that it would be wrong for you two to speak of me when I am gone? I cannot bear to think that you should deem it necessary to drive me from your memories, as one who had stepped in between your hearts. I am sure she will love you none the less for her remembrance of me, and therefore sometimes you will talk together of me, will you not?"

"Yes, we will often talk of you, for what dearer theme to both could we choose; what purer recollections could our memories cherish than of the friend we both loved so much, and who so well deserved our love?"

"And I am forgiven, Harold?"

"Were there aught to be forgiven, I would forgive; but I have never harbored in my most secret heart one trace of anger or resentment toward you. Do not talk more, dear Arthur. To-morrow, perhaps, you will be stronger, and then we will speak again. Here comes your mother, and she will scold me for letting you fatigue yourself so much."

"Raise me a little on the pillow, please. I seem to breathe more heavily to-night. Thank you, I will sleep now. Good night, mother; I will eat the gruel when I wake. I had rather sleep now. Good night, Harold!"

He fell into a slumber almost immediately, and they would not disturb him, although his mother had prepared the food he had been used to take.

"I think he is better to-night. He seems to sleep more tranquilly," said Mrs. Wayne. "If you will step below, I have got a dish of tea for you, and some little supper."

Harold went down and refreshed himself at the widow's neat and hospitable board, and then walked out into the evening, to dissipate, if possible, the cloud that was lowering about his heart. He paced up and down the avenue of willows, and though the fresh night air soothed the fever of his brain, he could not chase away the gloom that weighed upon his spirit. His mind wandered among mournful memories—the field of battle, strewn with the dying and the dead; the hospital where brave suffering men were groaning under the surgeon's knife; the sick chamber, where his friend was dying.

"And I, too," he thought, "have become the craftsman of Death, training my arm and intellect to be cunning in the butchery of my fellows! Wearing the instrument of torture at my side, and using the faculties God gave me to mutilate His image. Yet, from the pulpit and the statesman's chair, and far back through ages from the pages of history, precept and example have sought to record its justification, under the giant plea of necessity. But is it justified? Has man, in his enlightenment, sufficiently studied to throw aside the hereditary errors that come from the past, clothed in barbarous splendors to mislead thought and dazzle conscience? Oh, for one glimpse of the Eternal Truth! to teach us how far is delegated to mortal man the right to take away the life he cannot give. When shall the sword be held accursed? When shall man cease to meddle with the most awful prerogative of his God? When shall our right hands be cleansed forever from the stain of blood, and homicide be no longer a purpose and a glory upon earth? I shudder when I look up at the beautiful serenity of this autumn sky, and remember that my deed has loosened an immortal soul from its clay, and hurled it, unprepared, into its Maker's presence. My conscience would rebuke my hand, should it willfully shatter the sculptor's marble wrought into human shape, or deface the artist's ideal pictured upon canvas, or destroy aught that is beautiful and costly of man's ingenuity and labor. And yet these I might replace with emptying a purse into the craftsman's hand.

But will my gold recall the vital spark into those cold forms that, stricken by my steel or bullet, are rotting in their graves? The masterpiece of God I have destroyed. His image have I defaced; the wonderful mechanism that He alone can mold, and molded for His own holy purpose, have I shattered and dismembered; the soul, an essence of His own eternity, have I chased from its alotted earthly home, and I rely for my justification upon—what?—the fact that my victim differed from me in political belief. Must the hand of man be raised against the workmanship of God because an earthly bond has been sundered? Our statesmen teach us so, the ministers of our faith pronounce it just; but, oh God! should it be wrong! When the blood is hot, when the heart throbs with exaltation, when martial music swells, and the war-steed prances, and the bayonets gleam in the bright sunlight—then I think not of the doubt, nor of the long train of horrors, the tears, the bereavements, the agonies, of which this martial magnificence is but the vanguard. But now, in the still calmness of the night, when all around me and above me breathes of the loveliness and holiness of peace, I fear. I question nature, hushed as she is and smiling in repose, and her calm beauty tells me that Peace is sacred; that her Master sanctions no discords among His children. I question my own conscience, and it tells me that the sword wins not the everlasting triumph,—that the voice of war finds no echo within the gates of heaven."

Ill-comforted by his reflections, he returned to the quiet dwelling, and entered the chamber of his friend.

CHAPTER XXX.

The sufferer was still sleeping, and Mrs. Wayne was watching by the bedside. Harold seated himself beside her, and gazed mournfully upon the pale, still features that already, but for the expression of pain that lingered there, seemed to have passed from the quiet of sleep to the deeper calm of death.

"Each moment that I look," said Mrs. Wayne, wiping her tears away, "I seem to see the grey shadows of the grave stealing over his brow. The doctor was here a few moments before you came. The minister, too, sat with him all the morning. I know from their kind warning that I shall soon be childless. He has but a few hours to be with me. Oh, my son! my son!"

She bent her head upon the pillow, and wept silently in the bitterness of her heart. Harold forebore to check that holy grief; but when the old lady, with Christian resignation, had recovered her composure, he pressed her to seek that repose which her aged frame so much needed.

"I will sit by Arthur while you rest awhile; you have already overtasked your strength with vigil. I will awake you should there be a change."

She consented to lie upon the sofa, and soon wept herself to sleep, for she was really quite broken down with watching. Everything was hushed around, save the monotones of the insects in the fields, and the breathing of those that slept. If there is an hour when the soul is lifted above earth and communes with holy things, it is in the stillness of the country night, when the solitary watcher sits beside the pillow of a loved one, waiting the coming of the dark angel, whose footsteps are at the threshold. Harold sat gazing silently at the face of the invalid; sometimes a feeble smile would struggle with the lines of suffering upon the pinched and haggard lineaments, and once from the white lips came the murmur of a name, so low that only the solemn stillness made the sound palpable—the name of Oriana.

Toward midnight, Arthur's breathing became more difficult and painful, and his features changed so rapidly that Harold became fearful that the end was come. With a sigh, he stepped softly to the sofa, and wakened Mrs. Wayne, taking her gently by the hand which trembled in his grasp. She knew that she was awakened to a terrible sorrow—that she was about to bid farewell to the joy of her old age. Arthur opened his eyes, but the weeping mother turned from them; she could not bear to meet them, for already the glassy film was veiling the azure depths whose light had been so often turned to her in tenderness.

"Give me some air, mother. It is so close—I cannot breathe."

They raised him upon the pillow, and his mother supported the languid head upon her bosom.

"Arthur, my son! are you suffering, my poor boy?"

"Yes. It will pass away. Do not grieve. Kiss me, dear mother."

He was gasping for breath, and his hand was tightly clasped about his mother's withered palm. She wiped the dampness from his brow, mingling her tears with the cold dews of death.

"Is Harold there?"

"Yes, Arthur."

"You will not forget? And you will love and guard her well?"

"Yes, Arthur."

"Put away the sword, Harold; it is accursed of God. Is not that the moonlight that streams upon the bed?"

"Yes. Does it disturb you, Arthur?"

"No. Let it come in. Let it all come in; it seems a flood of glory."

His voice grew faint, till they could scarce hear its murmur. His breathing was less painful, and the old smile began to wreathe about his lips, smoothing the lines of pain.

"Kiss me, dear mother! You need not hold me. I am well enough—I am happy, mother. I can sleep now."

He slept no earthly slumber. As the summer air that wafts a rose-leaf from its stem, gently his last sigh stole upon the stillness of the night. Harold lifted the lifeless form from the mother's arms, and when it drooped upon the pillow, he turned away, that the parent might close the lids of the dead son.

THE END.

A LIST OF
BOOKS
ISSUED BY

CARLETON, PUBLISHER,
(LATE RUDD & CARLETON,)

413 Broadway,

NEW YORK.

NEW BOOKS

And New Editions Recently Issued by

CARLETON, PUBLISHER,

(LATE RUDD & CARLETON.)

418 *BROADWAY, NEW YORK.*

N.B.—THE PUBLISHER, upon receipt of the price in advance, will send any of the following Books, by mail, POSTAGE FREE, to any part of the United States. This convenient and very safe mode may be adopted when the neighboring Booksellers are not supplied with the desired work. State name and address in full.

The Cloister and the Hearth.
A magnificent new historical novel, by Charles Reade, author of "Peg Woffington," "Christie Johnstone," etc., etc., $1.25.

A Book about Doctors.
An amusing, entertaining, and gossipy volume about the medical profession—with many anecdotes. From English ed., $1.50.

Rutledge.
A powerful new American novel, by an unknown author, $1.25.

The Sutherlands.
The new novel by the popular author of "Rutledge," $1.25.

The Habits of Good Society.
A hand-book for ladies and gentlemen. Best, wittiest, most entertaining work on taste and good manners ever printed, $1.25.

The Great Tribulation.
Or, Things coming on the earth, by Rev. John Cumming, D.D., author "Apocalyptic Sketches," etc., two series, each $1.00.

The Great Preparation.
Or, Redemption draweth nigh, by Rev. John Cumming, D.D., author "The Great Tribulation," etc., two series, each $1.00.

Teach us to Pray.
A new devotional work on The Lord's Prayer, by Rev. John Cumming, D.D., author "The Great Tribulation," etc., $1.00.

Love (L'Amour).
A remarkable and celebrated volume on Love, translated from the French of M. J. Michelet, by Dr. J. W. Palmer, $1.00.

Woman (La Femme).
A continuation of "Love (L'Amour)," by same author, $1.00.

The Sea (La Mer).
New work by Michelet, author "Love" and "Woman," $1.00.

The Moral History of Women.
Companion to Michelet's "L'Amour," from the French, $1.00.

Mother Goose for Grown Folks.
A *brochure* of humorous and satirical rhymes for old folks, based upon the famous "Mother Goose Melodies," illustrated, 75 cts.

The Adventures of Verdant Green.
A rollicking humorous novel of English College life and experiences at Oxford University, with nearly 200 illus., $1.00.

The Old Merchants of New York.
Being entertaining reminiscences and recollections of ancient mercantile New York City, by "Walter Barrett, clerk," $1.50.

The Culprit Fay.
Joseph Rodman Drake's faery poem, elegantly printed, 50 cts.

Doctor Antonio.
One of the very best love-tales of Italian life ever published, by G. Ruffini, author of "Lorenzo Benoni," etc., etc., $1.25.

Lavinia.
A new love-story, by the author of "Doctor Antonio," $1.25.

Dear Experience.
An amusing Parisian novel, by author "Doctor Antonio," $1.00.

The Life of Alexander Von Humboldt.
A new and popular biography of this *savant*, including his travels and labors, with an introduction by Bayard Taylor, $1.25.

The Private Correspondence of Von Humboldt
With Varnhagen Von Ense and other European celebrities, $1.25.

Artemus Ward.
The best writings of this humorous author—illustrations, $1.00.

Beatrice Cenci.
An historical novel by F. D. Guerrazzi, from the Italian, $1.25.

Isabella Orsini.
An historical novel by the author of "Beatrice Cenci," $1.25.

The Spirit of Hebrew Poetry.
A new theological work by Isaac Taylor, author "History of Enthusiasm," etc.—introduction by Wm. Adams D.D., $2.00.

Cesar Birotteau.
The first of a series of selections from the best French novels of Honore de Balzac. Translated from the latest Paris editions by O. W. Wight and Frank B. Goodrich ("Dick Tinto"), $1.00.

Petty Annoyances of Married Life.
The second of the series of Balzac's best French novels, $1.00.

The Alchemist.
The third of the series of Balzac's best French novels, $1.00.

Eugenie Grandet.
The fourth of the series of Balzac's best French novels, $1.00.

The National School for the Soldier.
An elementary work for the soldier; teaching by questions and answers, thorough military tactics, by Capt. Van Ness, 50 cts.

The Partisan Leader.
The notorious Disunion novel, published at the South many years ago—then suppressed—now reprinted, 2 vols. in 1, $1.00.

A Woman's thoughts about Women.
A new and one of her best works, by Miss Mulock, author of "John Halifax, Gentleman," "A Life for a Life," etc., $1.00.

Ballad of Babie Bell.
Together with other poems by Thomas Bailey Aldrich, 75 cts.

The Course of True Love
Never did run smooth, a poem by Thomas B. Aldrich, 50 cts.

Poems of a Year.
By Thomas B. Aldrich, author of "Babie Bell," &c., 75 cts.

Curiosities of Natural History.
An entertaining and gossiping volume on beasts, birds, and fishes, by F. T. Buckland; two series, ea. sold separately, $1.25.

The Diamond Wedding.
And other miscellaneous poems, by Edmund C. Stedman, 75 cts.

The Prince's Ball.
A satirical poem by E. C. Stedman, with illustrations, 50 cts.

A Life of Hugh Miller.
Author of "Testimony of the Rocks," &c., new edition, $1.25.

Eric; or, Little by Little.
A capital tale of English school-life, by F. W. Farrar, $1.00.

Lola Montez.
Her lectures and autobiography, steel portrait, new ed., $1.25.

Spots on the Sun.
Or; The Plumb-Line papers, by Rev. T. M. Hopkins, $1.00

Tom Tiddler's Ground.
Charles Dickens's Christmas Story for 1861, paper cover, 25 cts.
National Hymns.
An essay by Richard Grant White. 8vo. embellished, $1.00.
George Brimley.
Literary essays reprinted from the British Quarterlies, $1.25.
The Kelly's and the O'Kelly's.
Novel by Anthony Trollope, author of "Doctor Thorne," $1.25.
General Nathaniel Lyon.
The life and political writings of this patriot soldier, $1.00.
Twenty Years Around the World.
A volume of travel by John G. Vassar, Poughkeepsie, $2.50.
Philip Thaxter.
A new American novel, one vol. 12mo., cloth bound, $1.00.
Nothing to Wear.
A satirical poem by Wm. A. Butler, with illustrations, 50 cts.
Political History of New York.
By Jabez B. Hammond, LL.D., 3 vols. steel portraits, $6.00.
Vernon Grove.
A novel by Mrs. Caroline H. Glover, Charleston, S. C., $1.00.
The Book of Chess Literature.
A complete Encyclopædia of this subject, by D. W. Fiske, $1.50.
From Haytime to Hopping.
A novel by the author of "Our Farm of Four Acres," $1.00.
Miles Standish, Illustrated.
Longfellow's poem with illustrations by J. W. Ehninger, $6.00.
The Afternoon of Unmarried Life.
An interesting theme admirably treated, new edition, $1.25.
Fast Day Sermons
Of 1861, the best Sermons by the prominent Divines, $1.25.
A Guide to Washington.
A complete hand-book for the National Capitol, illus., $1.00.
Doesticks' Letters.
The original letters of this great humorist, illustrated, $1.25.
Plu-ri-bus-tah.
A comic history of America, by "Doesticks," illus., $1.25.
The Elephant Club.
A humorous view of club-life, by "Doesticks," illus., $1.25.
The Witches of New York.
Comic adventures among fortune tellers, by "Doesticks," $1.25.

Fort Lafayette.
A novel by the Hon. Benjamin Wood of New York, $1.00.

The Mexican Papers.
In five separate parts; by Edward E. Dunbar, per set, $1.00.

Debt and Grace.
The Doctrine of a Future Life by Rev. C. F. Hudson, $1.25.

Thessalonica.
Or; the model church, by H. L. Hastings, 12mo., 75 cts.

Poems by E. G. Holland.
Niagara, and other poems; in blue and gold binding, 75 cts.

Wild Southern Scenes.
A tale, by the author of "Wild Western Scenes," $1.25.

Sybelle
And other poems by L——, blue and gold binding, 75 cts.

The Spuytenduyvil Chronicle.
A novel of fashionable life and society in New York, 75 cts.

Ballads of the War.
A collection of poems for 1861, by George W. Hewes, 75 cts.

Hartley Norman.
A new and striking American novel; one large 12mo., $1.25.

The Vagabond.
Sketches on literature, art, and society, by Adam Badeau, $1.00.

Emeline Sherman Smith.
A collection of selected poems, large octavo, elegant, $2.00.

Edgar Poe and his Critics.
A literary critique by Mrs. Sarah Helen Whitman, 75 cts.

The New and the Old.
Sketches in California and India, by Dr. J. W. Palmer, $1.25.

Up and Down the Irrawaddi.
Adventures in the Burman Empire, by J. W. Palmer, $1.00.

Sarah Gould.
A volume of miscellaneous poems, in blue and gold, 75 cts.

Cosmogony;
Or, the mysteries of creation, by Thomas A. Davies, $1.50.

An Answer to Hugh Miller
And other kindred geologists, by Thomas A. Davies, $1.25.

Walter Ashwood.
A novel by "Palu Siogvolk," author of "Schediasms," $1.00.

Southwold.
A new society novel by Mrs. Lillie Devereux Umsted, $1.00.

Brown's Carpenter's Assistant.
A practical work on architecture, with plans, large 4to., $5.00.

Two Ways to Wedlock.
A novelette reprinted from the N. Y. Home Journal, $1.00.

A Tribute to Kane,
And other poems, by Geo. W. Chapman, Milwaukee, 75 cts.

Ethel's Love Life.
A love-story by Mrs. Margaret J. M. Sweat, Portland, $1.00.

Recollections of the Revolution.
A private journal and diary of 1776, by Sidney Barclay, $1.00.

Poems by Flash.
A collection of poems by Henry L. Flash, Mobile, 75 cts.

Romance of a Poor Young Man.
A capital novel from the French of Octave Feuillet, $1.00.

A New Monetary System.
Or; rights of labor and property, by Edward Kellogg, $1.00.

Wa-Wa-Wanda.
A legend of old Orange County, New York, in verse, 75 cts.

Flirtation
And what comes of it. A play, by Frank B. Goodrich, 25 cts.

Blanche.
A legend in verse, by Sarah W. Brooks, Providence, 50 cts.

Husband vs. Wife.
A satirical poem, by Henry Clapp, Jr., illus. by Hoppin, 60 cts.

Roumania.
Travels in Eastern Europe by J. O. Noyes, illustrated, $1.50.

The Christmas Tree.
A volume of miscellany for the young, with illustrations, 75 cts.

The Captive Nightingale.
A charming little book for children, many illustrations, 75 cts.

Sunshine through the Clouds.
Comprising stories for juveniles, beautifully illustrated, 75 cts.

Abraham Lincoln.
A popular life of Lincoln and Hamlin, pamphlet, 25 cts.

John C. Fremont.
A popular life of Fremont and Dayton, pamphlet, 25 cts.

James Buchanan.
A popular life of Buchanan and Breckenridge, pamphlet, 25 cts.

John Bell.
A popular life of Bell and Everett, pamphlet covers, 25 cts.

www.ingramcontent.com/pod-product-compliance
Lightning Source LLC
Chambersburg PA
CBHW030235240426
43663CB00037B/835